C000202892

D...ny

Destiny

Andy, Chris, Rob and Ronald Frost

Authentic

10 09 08 07 06 05 04   7 6 5 4 3 2 1

First published in 2004 by Authentic Media
9 Holdom Avenue, Bletchley, Milton Keynes, Bucks., MK1 1QR, UK
and P.O. Box 1047, Waynesboro, GA 30830-2047, USA
www.authenticmedia.com

British Library Cataloguing in Publication Data

A catalogue record for this book is available from the British
Library

ISBN 1-85078-492-2

Cover design by Pete Barnsley
Print Management by Adare Carwin
Printed and Bound in Denmark by Nørhaven Paperback

Contents

Acknowledgements

With thanks to Jacqui Frost for supporting us all, to Ali Hull as desk editor, and to Camille Troughton for help with the manuscript.

Preface

by Roger Forster
(Founder of Ichthus Church Network)

Destiny is a book about generations. In this it emulates its more famous predecessor and indeed mentor, the Bible. The Scriptures' magnificent introduction 'In the beginning God created . . .' is followed by fifty chapters divided by eleven headings 'These are the generations (Hebrew) of . . .' followed by a name.

God is clearly interested in generations. He had the idea first and made humankind that way. He even reveals his special name to us in terms of three generations. 'I am the God of Abraham, Isaac and Jacob' Exodus 3:14–15. Genealogies abound in the Old Testament while the New Testament begins with 'The book of the generations (genealogy) of Jesus Christ.' Even the spiritual community, the church family, is viewed in generations. The Apostle John writes to fathers, young men and children. In presenting us with insights from three generations of one family Rob Frost has employed a fundamental feature of God's creative mind.

I am fascinated by this book with its histories and opinions of the three generations of the Frosts, interacting and discussing their common love and faith in Christ from their diversified backgrounds. This is because I have a few points of personal contact in these generations and their locations. But even without these the material presented is of such enormous importance for the ongoing of society and church that all of us will be intrigued and benefited from these interactive monologues and will find inspiration here to build another integrated company of people, which is the church.

My own personal interest is because the Frosts' own mission and Methodist Church involvement in South East London was so well known to me; even reaching back a further two generations to Rob's great-grandfather and his grandfather. Nevertheless even though I am able to be impressed by five generations of lovers of God and their works for him, the average reader only engages with three. However to be aware of the fact that four generations at least of godliness and prayer precede Andy's and Chris' (Rob's sons) passion for Jesus, is as impressive (if not more so) as the great missionary Hudson Taylor's story, which begins three generations before his conversion; his great-grandfather incidentally, being converted to Christ on his wedding day!

I first encountered the Frost dynasty when I was twelve years of age. Of course the Rob Frost of Easter People and Premier Radio and so on, was not yet even thought of, let alone around for me to run into, but great-grandfather Frost was. Many Sunday evenings when my parents, brother and I would walk a mile down the road to the Methodist church which then stood on that part of the South Circular road which passes through the borough of Lewisham, we would fall into step with a small white-haired old gentleman and his taller wife. At that age I was very sceptical, critical and omniscient as one is, especially of the church people with whom we all would soon congregate. Perhaps because I was having to attend with the family, I fulminated like an Old Testament prophet against the hypocrisy of this part of the body of Christ with whom we would soon be worshipping, but I was forced to admit to my family that if there was anyone at that church with the real thing – if Christianity were real – then Old Man Frost had got it. This dear, venerable little man who walked purposefully yet serenely along with us, communicated across at least seventy years to my boyish apprehension, a glow of spiritual well being and attractive holiness together with a love for a Creator and Saviour. I never over the years forgot Old Man Frost, as we boys cheekily called him, and the impression he left on me of the attractiveness of God.

Thirty-five years or so later, on a plane for Manila, I said to Rob 'Is Frost a Methodist name?' The impression

Rob (as baby) with left to right, Ronald William Frost (father), William Henry Forst (Grandfather) and Henry George Frost (Great Grandfather)

Mr Frost had left on me was still effective all that time later. It was then Rob told me I must have met his great-grandfather. The Rotherhithe mission hall, and the area of Bellingham and its Congregational church where grandfather Frost ministered, as well as Bermondsey Central Hall mentioned by father Frost, are all areas in which I have ministered myself. Rob himself has never ceased to amaze me with his evangelistic zeal and imaginative works of God and to evoke my highest admiration, while his boys Andy and Chris are an energetic addition, following their parents' creative communication skills, and give great hope for the future of the church in the United Kingdom.

So, welcome to the *Destiny* dynasty and its saga, but be aware of the last words of the Old Testament, which are that God 'will restore the hearts of the fathers to their children and the hearts of the children to their fathers so that I will not come and smite the land with a curse' (Mal. 4:6). God's destiny for humankind is restored relationships for the generations or otherwise a curse. Society, and sadly at times even the church, seem determined to head for the curse. This book offers and illustrates the possibility of the reverse of this mad Gaderene rush to destruction. There is hope; relationships can be restored and generations love and serve one another to mutual enrichment. Not only because the Frosts have done it but God is for it – he will restore his promises. Everything in God is for a restored humanity. Not a Freudian father-hating society but a Frost-like Heavenly Fathered community living out Jesus through all the generations.

Journey to Faith

From: Rob Frost
To: Ronald Frost
CC: Andy Frost; Chris Frost
Subject: Journey to Faith

Dear Dad, Andy and Chris,

We are three generations. We have lived through different times and known different experiences. We live in an age in which there is much misunderstanding between the generations, and at a time when the generations rarely speak to each other.

Dad, you have served the Lord in ministry for over sixty years. You knew life in the London Blitz, and a British church which dominated the social scene. I've now been an ordained minister for nearly thirty years, and I saw the swinging sixties and have witnessed a church in steady decline throughout my life. Andy and Chris, you're both starting out in Christian ministry – and you're part of Gen X and postmodern culture – and you're into a radical view of church which is sometimes hard for me to comprehend!

We've all been shaped by the world we've known, and so we all view things very differently. But we share a lot in common, too: our faith in Jesus Christ: our commitment to the mission of the Church: our sense of Christian optimism that God is working everything out.

We need to talk to each other. Not just because we're family, but because we represent three different generations. We need to understand where each of us is coming from . . . so that perhaps we can shed some light on where we're heading. Strange as it may seem, although we've talked a lot, we've never shared some of these deepest and most important areas of our lives. Maybe we've all been too busy, or too embarrassed, or too preoccupied with the trivia of everyday life.

So, here goes. An e-mail conversation in which we can say what we think, and share the deep stuff which makes up life and faith. I'll bare my soul, if you will

'Mum used to take me on her preaching engagements.'

yours. And, as we share, maybe we'll say something across three generations that we couldn't say from our own generation alone.

My Mum told me that when I was a few months old she used to take me on her preaching engagements. Apparently, when I cried, she would rock my carrycot with her foot in the pulpit, in the hope that I would go to sleep! I don't know if you remember those days, Dad, but it seemed a happy and stable home into which I came. I am deeply grateful for the Christian atmosphere in which I grew; for the daily prayers at my bedside, and for the encouragement to serve the Lord which you and Mum constantly gave me.

The time came when I became bored and fed up with church life. As a teenager I preferred to ride my bike around the park than be in Sunday school. I had been taken to church since my earliest childhood days, and I guess that I'd had about as much of it as I could take. My cherished memories of Sunday school are of the pranks I played rather than the lessons I learned. I remember being told to stand in the corridor in my primary class for mucking up the Lord's Prayer; and I got into trouble in the senior group for tying a girl's long pony-tail to the chair back!

I knew just about everything about Christianity by my mid-teens, but I hadn't met the Saviour. I had been to so many church meetings that I knew the Bible well, but I didn't really know Jesus at all. One weekend the youth group that I belonged to (the Central Hall Young People's Society . . . CHYPS for short) went on a camp to the village of Alvechurch, just outside Birmingham.

It was there that I began to see beyond my Sunday school religion. One evening, after a barbecue, in the quietness of the woods, I prayed, 'I'm not sure if I can accept it all or believe it all, Lord . . . but if you are real, show me.' That was when I began to move from a vague kind of belief in God to a living faith in Jesus Christ. It was a slow journey, and it took nearly a whole year; a period of much discussion, study and prayer.

First, I had to accept intellectually that Jesus existed as a real person. I read up on history and began to discover that there was evidence for Christ's life and ministry in the writings of early Jewish historians such as Josephus. At the teenage discussion group I went to, I started out as the argumentative sceptic in the group, but I gradually became more and more convinced that Jesus was someone very special. I remember the words of Peter making a particular impression on me: 'We have not depended on made-up stories in making known to you the mighty coming of our Lord Jesus Christ. With our own eyes we saw his greatness. We were there when he was given honour and glory by God the Father' (2 Pet. 1: 16–17).

I began to realise that Jesus was far more than just a 'nice guy'. And the more I asked questions about him and heard about him, the more I wanted to know him in a real way myself. I came to see that no one throughout history could be compared to him; the effect of his life on individuals and on nations has been immeasurable. Here was someone who not only preached forgiveness, but who hung on a cross to prove it!

Some of my Christian friends convinced me to take Jesus seriously, and to search for him with all my heart. As I met more and more believers, I began to want the kind of relationship with Jesus that they so obviously had. I knew that my intellectual assent was not enough because I hadn't really put my faith in him.

Things came to a head when we went back to the youth camp at Alvechurch at Easter. On Easter Sunday morning I heard a very elderly deaconess preach about the risen Jesus, and the story of the resurrection suddenly made sense to me. After lunch I took time out from the rest of the group and went for a walk in the woods. I found the same place in the wood where I had prayed before, but this time I prayed, 'Lord, I give you my life. All that I am, and all I ever hope to be.' I knelt and asked Jesus Christ to be my Friend and Saviour.

For the first time I glimpsed the reality of a living Saviour who had died for me and who could enter my life in a new and powerful way. There was no dramatic experience – just a new sense of peace and closeness to Jesus. Before this act of submission Jesus seemed far away, high up – as if on the mountaintop. He was distant and unknowable, and he couldn't even be reached in prayer. But when I came to know Jesus for myself, he came down from the mountaintop and began to walk the valley by my side. He became my personal Friend – always there to share whatever joys or sorrows might come my way. There, in the stillness of the forest, I met Jesus Christ. And for the first time I believed his great promise: 'I will never leave you nor forsake you.' I took him at his word.

Soon afterwards I stuck a sign on my bedroom door which read, 'Tell Jesus.' Whenever I went out of the door I couldn't help but see it. Sometimes I went out of the door to sit an exam, and was enduring that awful nerve-racking feeling that precedes exams! As I went out the sign reminded me to 'tell Jesus.' At other times I went out of the door feeling great as I was going to meet my girlfriend. The sign reminded me that in every situation Jesus was there to share my life with me. I came to understand that knowing Jesus is what real Christianity is all about.

My relationship with Jesus is now at the centre of my life. There have been many times when I've failed him and let him down, but he has never let go of me, and he's always brought me back.

And so I really am very grateful for my upbringing, Dad. I know that there were many pressures on you and Mum when I was a child. You were leading very large churches with many hundreds in the congregation. You had pastoral responsibilities that were heavier than most ministers today could ever understand. And there were financial pressures on you that meant it was a genuine struggle to make ends meet. Yet you both had time for me, and you always supported me and encouraged me in whatever madcap scheme I was into. I will never forget how you would take me rowing on the River Yealm near Plymouth every Saturday afternoon, even though you were sometimes composing the next day's sermon as I rowed!

You created a home where faith was real, where the Lord was not only talked about but talked to, and where Christian living seemed the most natural way of life of all. When I rebelled against the faith and against the church, I knew how disappointed you were, and yet you were not too harsh with me. Above all, you gave me the context in which I could find a living faith in Jesus, and that has been the most precious gift of all.

I fear that I didn't do so well for you, Andy and Chris. I really struggled as a parent, and during your teenage years I have to confess that I found parenting the hardest thing I've done in my whole life. So what happened that changed you both so dramatically? In all the years we've known each other we've never shared our faith stories with each other. I've never really heard your testimony, either, Dad. Perhaps, by sharing this journey of faith with each other we'll see that though much has changed across these three generations, the journey to faith is still much the same. . .

Love,
Rob

From: Ronald Frost
To: Rob Frost
CC: Andy Frost; Chris Frost
Subject: Journey to Faith

Dear Robert,

My Christian journey began over thirty years before yours. I was at school when the teacher said 'There is more than one meaning to the word "Jubilee"' to forty fifteen year old boys in the autumn of 1935. In an attempt to divert his attention from the half hour's Bible study with which every school day was supposed to commence at that time, the biggest boy in the form had asked him about the posters that were appearing all over South London advertising a visit of 'The Jubilee Singers'.

The comment was of particular interest to me, because I had been one of the ten boys who had been fortunate enough to be selected to go to the Mall in the May of that year to witness the Silver Jubilee procession of their Majesties King George V and his consort, Queen Mary. Neither I nor any of my class-mates could see any connection between this event, that had enthralled the whole nation, and the placards being displayed so many months later, stating that these Jubilee Singers were to perform each evening for ten days at the Lewisham Town Hall.

Far from preventing the Scripture lesson that morning, the enquiry simply led to the order, 'Get your Bibles out and turn to Leviticus chapter 25.' Oh dear! Where was Leviticus? At last the noise caused by everyone trying to advise everyone else how to find this Old Testament book subsided, and we began to read round the class, verse by verse. As we proceeded, it was explained to us that the first meaning of the word Jubilee was 'a trumpet blast'. Then we were told it was related to the word 'Jubilation', it could be any joyful celebration. It was pointed out that one of the main causes for happiness in the Old Testament was that every fifty years the slaves had to be set free.

Therefore the significance of the Jubilee Singers was that they were all people who had been born in the southern states of North America into families that had been slaves. The laws passed in Britain and America during the nineteenth century had given freedom to these people, so they now toured the world to express their joy – the jubilation of their families.

When my particular school friend and I heard that these twelve men and women would all have black skins, because their forebears had been captured from the coastal lands of West Africa, we decided that we must go and see them. To see such people in London in those days was so rare that they proved to be a great attraction. Apart from the British Empire exhibition at Wembley in 1926, I think that I had previously only ever seen one person without a white skin. Therefore to see twelve of them all at once, night after night, was something not to be missed. The fact that one did not have to pay to go in was an added attraction.

Of course we enjoyed their rendering of all the traditional Negro spirituals, but did not realise at the time that they were only there to make sure that all the seats in the town hall were filled, so that Mr. Lindsey Glegg, an evangelist hired by the National Young Life campaign, would have a full house to whom he could deliver his gospel message. No one – least of all we schoolboys - wanted to hear a preacher, but once the crowd was attracted by the Jubilee Singers, the evangelist made good use of his opportunity and, with superb oratory each evening, pleaded for those present to 'Accept Christ.'

On the second Monday night I did just that. We were asked to sing the last hymn sitting down, but to stand up if we wanted to signify that we were prepared to commit our lives to Jesus. The hymn was,

> All to Jesus I surrender,
> All to Him I freely give,
> I will ever love and serve Him
> In His presence daily live,
> I surrender all, I surrender all,
> All to Thee, my blessed Saviour,
> I surrender all.

I don't think that it was only the speaker's brilliant Bible exposition that persuaded me to take that step – which I have never regretted – it was also the presence of the Jubilee Singers. They were not only an attraction guaranteed to bring people to the venue; the message of their songs emphasised the whole purpose of the mission.

Further, almost every night one of them gave their personal testimony. To hear how Christ had sustained them in all the privations of their lives gave the guarantee that no matter what life might hold for me, Christ would be sufficient. Much was made of the idea that being a redeemed slave was nothing compared to being a redeemed sinner, through the price that Jesus had paid on the Cross.

Having been born into a dynamically Christian family, I was well immersed in the facts of the faith, but what had happened on that night was something different. I clearly remember riding to school on my bicycle the next morning, and whistling all the way. I was truly joyful. Until then everything had seemed so worrying, examinations were pending and within a few months I would be facing the need to get a job in a society where there was mammoth unemployment, but now the prospect appeared to be quite different. There was a peace that I had never experienced before.

Phrases like, 'Being born again', 'Being saved', 'Getting converted' all became more meaningful to me. I didn't understand all the theology of it, but I was sure – and have been sure ever since – that something spiritually significant had happened to me, and I could see no logical reason why it could not similarly happen to everyone else.

Perhaps I ought to say that my school friend did not stand up on that night, but soon afterwards was confirmed in a high Anglican church. He qualified as a doctor and after spending the Second World war in the R.A.M.C., went as a medical missionary to India, where he ultimately became Superintendent of the Vellore Hospital. Later, he said that he realised that the patients needed spiritual help even more than medical aid, and after a further period of study was ordained as a priest. His Christian pilgrimage has therefore been different from mine, but I am sure that it is none the less valid.

Coming to faith in Christ is not the same for everyone, but the opportunity is available to everyone. Jesus said, 'Whosoever believes on me shall not perish.' The word 'whosoever' excludes no one. Thank you for sharing your faith story with me . . . and now you know mine!

Best wishes,
Dad

From: Andy Frost
To: Rob Frost
CC: Ronald Frost; Chris Frost
Subject: Journey to Faith

Dear Rob,

Dad, I don't know if it was the same forty years ago when you were a child but today every minister's kid is expected to fit into one of two different categories. They are expected either to rebel against their parents, chuck in their faith and adopt a life of debauchery; or else they are expected to become weak, timid Christians who find faith through a process of osmosis so that they never really fit into any culture except churchianity.

All of my life, I have hated fitting into categories. Yet everyone around me, whether they knew it or not, seemed to be pushing me into one of these moulds. In my early teens, my school friends wanted me to choose the former, rebelling against Christianity. They wanted me truly to become one of them and put aside my beliefs. I too felt the urge to break free from the constraints of church culture and was desperate to be accepted. Yet I was so aware that I would be letting you down as well as all the people that had been involved in making me the person that I was – relatives, family friends and of course Grandad. Neither direction felt right but, as I approached the age of fifteen, I knew that a choice was on the horizon.

Life has never been normal, though I guess no family is. I think that our upbringing was slightly different to that of the average person. It still bemuses me how people have this funny idea of what it is to be brought up in the home of a Christian leader! They have this misconception that life is simple and easy – that we sit peacefully around the Sunday roast with beaming faces discussing theology, church and the happiness of family life. People see you on the stage and presume that life is always good, always nice, always godly – that arguments are an impossibility in the holy Frost residence.

Living under such an illusion was hard. Don't get me wrong. I do thank God for you and the whole family but it was not always as easy as people presumed. People always saw you as the perfect father and that was hard. I never wanted to bring your character into disrepute and the myth of family perfection lived on. The pressures on ministers' children, especially those in the national limelight, are rarely understood.

For example, no one understands what it was like when I sat in a packed church as you got up to speak. Whilst sitting at the back trying to appear anonymous with other disillusioned young people, my heart dreaded possible embarrassing illustrations. Then suddenly the words would come . . . 'It's a bit like my son . . . The illustration was poignant and the congregation were challenged yet meanwhile I was robbed of dignity, as the surrounding people looked over and laughed. It was even worse when you were doing our school assembly!

Or picture the pressure when complete strangers came up to me and say 'Oh . . . are you Rob Frost's son?' Immediately their minds constructed an image of who I was, based solely upon sermon illustrations and dated prayer letters. They felt that they had the right to interrogate me on my personal relationship with God. The reputation of the great Rob Frost was in the balance, dependent on my answers. The usual tack was to shrug them off with a minimal response but they were not satisfied and would pursue their line of questioning, desperate to gain more from their encounter with a Christian celebrity's son.

The constant questioning led to a series of perfected responses tailored to please the Christian ear.

Meanwhile, the true Andy Frost became a real mystery. I definitely believed in God – I always had and I could not deny my first memorable 'experience' of God, when I was aged seven. But God seemed so distant at church and in life generally. I think that when you grow up in a family that is full of love and grace, you sometimes take it for granted and fail to recognise what you really have.

Then perhaps the hardest part of childhood were the endless missions and preaches that you would go on – there was always a present to sweeten the tension but the Saturdays when the other fathers would be on the sideline cheering on their sons were always hard and the broken promises were painful. I guess this is common to many childhoods, with so many single parent families but in ours, ministry was normally given priority over a young boy's relationship with his father.

I don't want to paint the dark picture of an unloving father. There were special times too when I would

'There were special moments, too.'

journey with you around the country, eating junk food and talking about films, history and sex. I loved the way that you attempted to play football in the park even though you were often exhausted from the business of the office. I was thankful when you agreed to stop using me in illustrations. You were and still are one of my heroes but it wasn't always so easy.

So I started to live a lie – attending church and pretending to be a sorted Christian whilst secretly nurturing a hangover from the night before and trying to remember the girl's name that I had kissed. For a while it seemed to be the best solution – my parents were happy, the church was happy and my friends were happy.

Yet I was no longer happy and soon I could no longer keep up the fraud. Gradually the Sunday lie-ins became routine and the church services became more and more of an irregularity. I didn't want to miss out on the joys of living life and there was no attraction in cold church services. I respect the fact that you gave me the freedom to choose what to do with my life, that you allowed me to make the mistakes that I had to make. Those late teenage years were difficult for the whole family and our relationship was frequently tension-filled as Chris and Mum worked as the peacemakers. As I was becoming a man, the power struggle had started!

The years of partying must have really hurt you and I am so sorry for the pain that I have caused. In response to the endless mornings of cleaning up the sick from the night before, my abusive behaviour and the selfishness of my heart, you kept showing me grace. Throughout this time I knew God was real but it all seemed so distant. I kept going to the school Christian Union (probably unknown to you). But I found the local churches so patronising: they seemed to know me before I had even arrived. At the same time I was still fighting not to fit into the stereotypical Reverend's son role that I despised so greatly. I had chosen to go the first route – ditching my faith for hedonism. Yet God intervened with alternative plans!

At the age of eighteen I wanted to see the world and Camp America seemed like a good plan. As I filled in the application form there were three areas that I had to teach from a list of twenty. Soccer and drama were definites but the third was somewhat elusive. As I scanned the list, 'Bible Stories' seemed like a simple solution for the third option. With a lifetime of sermons, Sunday school lessons and missions - this was definitely an ability that I had!

Two months later and I was living on a Salvation Army summer camp which took many poor young people from the state of Washington and offered them a week full of sports, workshops and Jesus! Its aim was to evangelise all these kids and I was expected to lead them to him. It was as I was talking to young men from the inner city with gang tattoos down their arms that I realised just how blessed I had been. As these young people came to Jesus weeping, my heart was moved and I realised that believing in God was not enough – it was time to start being a disciple and following Jesus.

Probably the hardest thing as a young person was coming before you and realising that all along you had been right and I had been wrong. I had to humble myself and let go of my pride. This was perhaps the hardest thing!

Though I regret much of what I did in my rebellious years, those experiences gave me an understanding of the world that has made me the person that I am today. As I have matured as a Christian, I have gained in confidence so that now I know that I need not walk in my father's shadow: Jesus chose me for the man that I am.

Thanks for being my father,
Andy

From: Chris Frost
To: Rob Frost
CC: Ronald Frost; Andy Frost;
Subject: Journey to Faith

Dear Dad,

I'd like to share my story with you. I guess I had every-thing a kid could ask for: a loving family, close friends and a comfortable lifestyle. Everything had started swimmingly. The message of Jesus was given to me on Sunday mornings at Kids' club . . . a bit of fun but noth-ing with any real bite. I was carried along every week by you and Mum and can still remember all the great Bible stories I learnt, all the pretty pictures I drew and all the nice prayers I said but it never dawned on me that my Creator wanted to be intimate with me. Looking back, it seems that my teachers were scared of what a real faith would look like in someone so young.

At a very early age I felt the need to impress people. My two insecurities were my height (the lack of it!) and the fact that you Dad, were a full-blown Jesus freak. It was hard to respect the authority of a man that I really just didn't under-stand. It was therefore my prerogative to prove that I wasn't as sad as my Dad by breaking the identity I had inherited. The choices I made around the ages of eleven to thirteen slowly started to bring a veil over my eyes. I had grown into the seemingly harmless habits of drinking, smoking and taking pot. I can remember times at the age of twelve locked away from my friends in a toilet, sprawled over the seat with vomit on my mouth and tears in my eyes. It was so painful, feeling so lonely and so out of touch with who I really was.

All through this I was still visiting church. It seemed to give some sort of vague meaning to my life, but it was hard to keep up the lie that I was living there: either no one knew what me and my friends were dealing with or they just didn't feel they had the authority to address it. Then, just before my thirteenth birthday, the guys around my age at the church were asked to go on a week away and I eventually agreed. What seemed like a good opportunity to spend some time with a girl I fancied turned out to be a life-changing experience. At this camp my view of Christianity was transformed: I was starting to become aware of the reality of the leaders' faith. They didn't profess to have all the answers but they were really in love with Jesus, something that seemed quite bizarre to me at the time. What happened on the last night of that camp I will never forget.

It was the last meeting of the week and after a moving preach the band started playing some songs. As the music continued, it started to unlock something in my friends' hearts. My mind started racing. What was going on? Why were my macho mates weeping like girls? After twenty minutes or so, I had had enough and, in a very angry voice in my head, I shouted 'Come on then, God, if you're real show me, prove it to me . . . now!'. Suddenly a wave of power flowed over me. I tried to hide it but another and then another came. I didn't know what to do with myself so I ran outside and lay prostrate on the floor. Before I knew it there was a leader praying over me: 'In the name of Jesus leave this boy alone.' Suddenly I sensed there was a battle inside me and as the praying continued, I felt a demonic presence being shaken out of my legs. Eventually it was over and the most amazing feeling came over me. It was incredible: for the first time I could remember I was free, in control and loving every second of it. God in his amazing mercy had broken into my life and I knew he lived!

Going back home was hard, very hard. I felt I had been taken from one form of loneliness to another. There was no one I really felt I could share my experience with or from whom I could learn more about living the Christian life. Day by day I felt my faith weakening and my passion to do bad things increasing. Deep down I didn't want to turn back to my old ways but it was too hard to swim against the flow on my own.

The next five years of my life led me down a progressive spiral away from my faith and away from you Dad. Things kept getting worse and worse. By the age of eighteen I had been arrested for carrying drugs, started to have sex with my girlfriend and had become aggressive. I can remember punching the walls of my room so hard that my knuckles would bruise. There was so much hurt and pain bottled up inside: I knew I was running away from God but was just too scared to admit that I was wrong. I pretended I was in control, happy and content, but away from my friends, I was sad, cold-hearted and lonely. God kept reminding me about Himself, waiting there patiently but I was not ready.

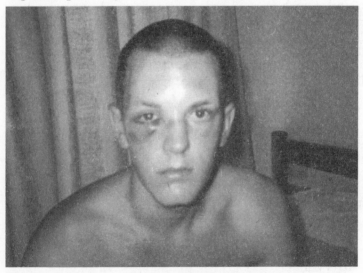

'I was ready, and God knew it.'

I remember that my life had gone into a real slump a couple of summers ago when I went on a 'lads' holiday with my mates. I knew you didn't want me to go but I did anyway and I bathed in sin there every day, getting recklessly drunk, using women and fighting. One day I can remember waking up and looking in front of a mirror. As I looked at my reflection, I saw my body covered in bruises and dry blood. My eyes seemed to echo emptiness. I wanted to cry but it was as if there were no tears inside. I lacked any hope and didn't really see the point in this life any more.

I was ready, and God knew it. I ended up going to Andy's mission in Newquay – and everything about Jesus started to make sense again. It wasn't until one of the last meetings that it all came together though. In the middle of a prolonged worship session, a man came up to me and declared that God had shown him my soul and that I needed to recommit my life to Jesus. Something just seemed to click and I agreed. Within seconds I was praying and was flooded with tears. All the hurt and pain I had felt for so long had come out. Jesus had brought light into the darkness, released me from the chains of sin and set me free!

Passages like 'what I once thought was valuable is worthless. Nothing is as wonderful as knowing Christ Jesus my Lord' (Phil. 3:7) and 'I am sure that neither death, nor life, nor angels, nor ruling spirits, nothing now, nothing in the future, nor anything else in the whole world will be able to separate me from the love of God that is in Christ Jesus my Lord' (Rom. 8:38,39), suddenly seemed to speak to me so profoundly.

Over the past couple of years I've become really proud of my Christian heritage and come to know why you brought me up as you did. Thanks Dad.

All my love
Chris

From: Rob Frost
To: Ron Frost
CC: Andy Frost; Chris Frost
Subject: Journey to Faith

Dear Dad, Andy and Chris,

Thanks for your e-mails.

The London you knew in your youth, Dad, is barely recognisable today. You grew up in a city of trams and horses and carts: monocultural in ethos, with thirty minutes of Bible study at school each morning.

I never knew that Lindsay Clegg was the evangelist who called you to faith. I heard him preach when I was nineteen. He seemed very elderly as he shuffled onto the platform at the Filey Convention, assisted by one of the others on the platform party. Yet even now I can remember the anointed way in which he prayed and the compelling power of his preaching.

I've always loved that hymn 'I surrender all', and I must have sung it a hundred times without ever knowing that it was your conversion hymn. I've used it quite a few times when I've made evangelistic appeals. It's funny how these things resonate down the years and speak the same message to different generations.

It seems really strange that I've known you all my life, but I never knew this story of your journey to faith. I guess that in some ways what happened during 'I surrender all' is still influencing us all nearly seventy years later.

Your e-mail is certainly honest, Andy. As I read about some of the pain you went through as a kid, I feel I failed you as a Dad in many ways. Looking back to the heady days when I was building my mission work, there were times when I was too preoccupied with my ministry, too caught up with other people, and too busy for you when you needed me. I'm really sorry for that.

I never stopped loving you, though. And the pressures of trying to hold together a national ministry and a lively family were sometimes pretty overwhelming. During your teenage years there were times when I was driven to total despair. I saw you heading down a road to self-destruction, and there seemed no way of stopping you. When I discussed this with my boss the Reverend Dr Donald English once, he simply said 'you've got to learn the art of hands-off parenting . . . just pray!' And that's all I could do. When we said goodbye to you at the airport as you left for your wild summer in the United States I dreaded to think what might happen.

When you called from the USA to say that you were praying for the kids in your camp, I literally couldn't believe it! And when you phoned asking for tips on

'I never stopped loving you, though.'

'how to preach' it seemed like a miracle! It all reminded me that God's hand was on you, even when I was a 'hands off' parent. I'm deeply grateful to God for the reconciliation which he has brought between us, and for the rich friendship we now have. I feel that we're making up for the years which we lost.

I can't begin to explain how worried I was about you, Chris. I recognise that I failed you, too, and looking back there are ways I would do parenting differently if I could have my time again. You seemed to be racing headlong down a road towards personal disaster. When you told me about your conversion on the mission in Newquay, I didn't know whether to laugh or cry: When in the next breath you announced that you were off with your mates to Amsterdam the next day, I didn't think you'd still be following Jesus when you got back.

I was wrong. You stuck to your new-found faith with a commitment that made you a real target on that holiday and you came back a stronger Christian than when you left. I know that I failed you as a father, too, and my thankfulness to God for what he's done in your life is indescribable.

One night we were standing on Newcastle station, and I was seeing you back on a train to university after you'd visited me on mission. You told me that you, too, had once resented all of my protracted periods away from home when I'd been away working. You went on to say 'but it's okay now, Dad, because I now understand why . . .'

From the Jubilee singers in London, to a youth group barbecue in Birmingham, and from Camp America in Seattle to breakdancing evangelists in Newquay . . . God has spoken to us. Each of us came to a point of decision in our journey to faith. Each of us made a choice. Each of us found our place in God's promises . . . we chose our destiny . . . and we followed Jesus.

My hope is that someone who shares this correspondence between us will find their place in God's promises . . . and choose their destiny, too.

God bless,
Rob

2

Call to Ministry

From: Rob Frost
To: Ronald Frost
CC: Andy Frost; Chris Frost
Subject: Call to Ministry

Dear Dad, Andy and Chris,

Many Christians struggle with the concept of 'the call of God', and I know that each of us has wrestled with a sense of 'call' and what it means in real life. For you, Dad, it has led to a lifetime of ordained ministry in a church denomination, but I sense that for both Andy and Chris this call is being interpreted in much looser and more unstructured ways. The call of Jesus to discover our gifts and to find our vocation has reached us all in different ways. I'm convinced that this sense of call which we all share goes far beyond something in our genes or the social conditioning of our upbringing. Ultimately it is about the transcendent Christ who speaks in different ways to each rising generation.

I can still remember my own vocational journey with real clarity. I somehow imagined that a call of God would, if it came to me, arrive as a neat package detailing where I was headed in the Lord's service and how to get there. No such package has arrived, however, and looking back across the years my call has been a series of struggles, questions, conversations and decisions that all seem much more significant in hindsight than they did at the time.

I had wanted to be a television producer from the age of thirteen. I had followed you, Dad, as you did the epilogues on Westward Television, and avidly attended outside broadcasts whenever possible to pick up whatever information I could. I borrowed books on audio recording, film production and television technology from the local library and read them with great interest. There was nothing else in the world that I wanted to do.

Soon after I became a Christian I managed to get a place at the Birmingham School of Photography and

'In Andy and Chris the "call" is being interpreted in more unstructured ways.'

Film, and was thrilled to have got my foot in the door of the industry I so wanted to work in. The course wasn't exactly what I'd hoped it would be, however, and I had to spend hours in the photo darkroom learning how to process and enlarge pictures. There were endless lectures on composition, and I had to learn how to photograph a bunch of bananas or a tea-set . . . or try to make a plate of fish and chips look edible!

One of the highlights of my year, however, included the opportunity to make a colour slide presentation about the meaning of Christmas . . . which involved taking countless pictures of 'Mary and Joseph' journeying across the Worcestershire countryside. In the final term I got to make a film, which featured a dramatic car-crash and asked deep questions about the meaning of life. Over the year it became clear that I was not really interested in the scientific processes of photography, but that I was much more focussed on discovering visual ways of communicating the Christian faith. I applied for a place at the Regent Street School of Film and TV and, against stiff competition, was accepted. It seemed that my long-standing ambition would be fulfilled at last.

Around Easter time, just five months before going away to the School of Film and Television, I went to camp with my youth group. It was a wonderful weekend, and on the Sunday morning I made a response at the morning service, offering my life to God. As I walked through the woods that Easter Sunday afternoon the closeness of Jesus was really tangible. I felt that he was calling me on to full-time Christian service, and life felt very exciting and on the edge. It was a very emotionally charged time for me, as I seriously began to wonder whether I could respond to such a call. Did it mean that I would have to give up my place at the School of Film and TV? Or could I combine this with some kind of ministry in future years?

I remember discussing this dilemma with my friends and parents, and everyone seemed to have a different take on it. God seemed silent on the matter. Things grew a bit clearer when I met a group of Cliff College students on a mission team, and as I heard their testimonies in a small town called Hinckley I really felt that I should give some quality time to seeking my vocation.

This concept was very new to me, but as I talked with these students they told me that they had given a year to God to study the Bible, to pray and to offer their future to the Lord. So I decided to do the same. I sold my most precious possession, my camera, and friends at church helped to sponsor me on this first step along my vocational road. The year at Cliff College was inspiring. It was definitely a watershed in my life. It was a year of studying the Bible, of preaching in tiny Derbyshire village chapels, of going out on missions and of enjoying quality worship and fellowship. These were all very helpful and maturing experiences for me.

One night stood out in that year of new Christian challenges. In October, we went out on mission to a place near Sheffield called Gleadless. I was appointed to go out onto the streets that dark, wet Saturday night and to invite people in to see a Billy Graham film starring a very young Cliff Richard.

I couldn't find anyone to come in, so, feeling rather a failure, I went into the fish and chip shop to get some chips. Three motorbikes roared up and three young lads sauntered in. Their leathers and crash helmets made them look very menacing. At last I summoned up the courage to invite them to the mission film night, and to my joy and amazement, they accepted!

They arrived at the film night after the movie had started. They sat on a table at the back flicking chewing gum and generally mucking around. When the film

ended and the lights went up, our team evangelist began
to speak and they all went very quiet. One of the motor-
bike lads, a nineteen year old, went forward, and was
led off to the counselling room where he prayed the
prayer of commitment to Jesus Christ. I was overjoyed
that I had brought this young man in from the street to
hear the gospel.

You can imagine, then, how devastated we all were
when next morning we heard that he had been killed in a
tragic motorcycle accident less than two hours after I'd
last seen him. It changed the whole course of our mission,
and in some ways that event changed the course of my
life. In that moment I became convinced that evangelism
isn't something which the church does to boost numbers,
or which it embarks on just now and again to raise its pro-
file. No, the commission of Jesus to us all is that we must
'Go into all the world and make disciples. . .' His command is at the heart of our faith and at the core of our
believing. God spoke to me   powerfully about my future
vocation through that experience. And, in some ways, I
can track my passion for reaching men and women with
the gospel to that tragic night in Sheffield.

That was only the beginning of my vocation journey,
however. I could tell of the huge struggles I had with
going into 'full-time' Christian work, of my painful road
towards ordination as a Methodist minister, and of my
long journey to becoming an ordained evangelist. I've
also learned that God seems to take life's experiences
and to weave them into a pattern for his glory. Some of
the things I learnt at the Birmingham School of
Photography and Film have come in very useful in my
work on radio and television – and even though at the
time I thought I'd been travelling down a dead end,
those lessons learned and skills gained have been very
useful down the years.

I have learned that call does not come in easy to open packages. My call has been shaped and formed by a thousand different experiences. Sometimes others have spotted things in me that they felt God could use and they've been used by God to guide me in one direction or another. At other times I've sensed a call, offered myself, and been rejected. I've knocked on doors that have remained firmly shut to me . . . and sometimes that's been hard to accept.

Even now, in middle age, I am still pursuing my call; exploring new avenues, discovering new gifts, testing new opportunities. My experience of call has lasted a lifetime, and even now I'm looking forward to the new surprises which I believe that God has in store for me. I'm sure that there are aspects of my vocation which God has yet to unfold.

As I look at what the Lord is doing in all of our lives at the moment I can see that we're all still on this vocational journey. You're a real example in this, Dad, because your own ministry has blossomed and developed in exciting new ways . . . even in your eighties! I'm sure that it's this journey which makes the Christian life so exciting. Jesus is calling us onward towards our full potential every day. And who knows what's next for any of us?

God bless,
Rob

From: Ronald Frost
To: Rob Frost
CC: Andy Frost; Chris Frost
Subject: Call to Ministry

Dear Robert,

I have had a particularly happy and satisfying life, and much of it has been because I felt called to be a Christian minister. At various stages of offering as a candidate for the Methodist ministry I was asked by different individuals and committees, 'How do you know you are called?' They seemed to doubt my sincerity, but to explain to them why I was so certain seemed an impossible task. There were times when I was terrified that they would turn me down, and yet I was quite sure in my own heart and mind that I was responding to a Divine invitation.

It all began when I was twelve years old. We had to write an essay at school one day on 'What I would like to be when I grow up.' Almost without thinking, I wrote that I would like to be a Free Church minister. This may have been because my Uncle Eric had just been ordained and I had heard my mother and father saying that his life would be very different from that of a motor mechanic, which had been his employment before going to Richmond College. If so, it was sub-conscious, for I had given little thought to the matter: the words just seemed to slip off the end of my pen. I got a very good mark for the essay, but it so impressed the English Teacher, Dickie Holland, that at the next school Open Day, he talked to my mother about it. Since I had never mentioned either the essay or its subject to anyone, she was most surprised and told me that I was aiming too high. She said that Uncle Eric was an exception, and that people in our stratum of society could not hope to enter the professions.

She emphasised that I was fortunate in attending the South London Institute of Commerce, and not any ordinary council school. Therefore I must be content at getting qualifications within the Royal Society of Arts and the London Chamber of Commerce, and be satisfied with getting a job in a bank or big business house, preferably as an accountant. This conversation, I knew, presented me with the realistic situation, but the idea never left me. That was strange, for our family did not attend a church where there was an ordained ministry. We, in fact, were an important part of a London City Mission Hall, Emmanuel Hall, in Lower Sydenham. My father was the Sunday school superintendent, and my mother ran the Sisterhood, a meeting for some thirty very poor women from one of the most destitute parts of South London.

Inevitably as time went on my sister became Sunday school pianist, and I sang in the choir. We went to the Mission every Sunday morning and every Sunday evening without fail, although it involved a walk of some two miles from the slightly better class area of Beckenham. Since the man in charge of this place was not an ordained minister, it seemed strange that I should have written so definitely about wanting to be ordained.

It is true that I did see such a person one Sunday morning a month. This was because I attended a Boy Scout Troop at the Bellingham Congregational church, where my sister and I went to Sunday school on Sunday afternoons. We had to go to church parade on the second Sunday morning of each month. There I saw a gowned minister with clerical collar, and it may have been the formal dignity of this man that impressed my young mind. Be that as it may, I cannot escape the fact that gradually the subject of the essay I had written at the age of twelve persisted in my mind. Then, when I was fifteen, I had the conversion experience, under the ministry of the lay evangelist Lindsey Glegg, which I have described in the previous chapter.

That was in October 1935. Early in January 1936, King George V died, and on the Sunday night when he was lying in state in Westminster Hall, we had a preacher at the Mission. He was a local wealthy business man called Stanley Gardner, and he took for his text, 'In the year that King Uzziah died, I saw the Lord . . . and he said, "Who shall I send and who will go for us?" Then I said, "Lord here am I; send me."'

That clinched the matter. Yet I could not see how I could become a minister. My education was pointing in an entirely different direction, my Christian involvement was not within one of the major denominations, and I really had no contact with any ordained minister as a role model, but that sermon clearly had said to me, 'In the year that King George V died you have seen the Lord and he is saying to you, "Who shall I send?" and you must respond "Lord here am I, send me."'

I had no idea how it could happen. I left school and started working in a Belgian shipping company, hoping to make progress in their finance department, so as to ultimately get my qualifications as a certified accountant. Then on Good Friday, 1938, when I was at the mission singing in the choir, my paternal grandparents called on my mother and father. When I got home I found the four of them at prayer. They were praying that the latest doings of Hitler would not result in war. When they had finished, they told me that the Methodist church in Rotherhithe, where my grandparents worked, had a problem, because all of their scout leaders had been called up to join the newly formed Militia, and that if they could not find at least one person to replace them, the troop would have to close down.

I was nearly eighteen, and not needed in the 7th Lewisham Troop where I had grown up, so I volunteered to go and help. So I got involved in Methodism; so I had the chance to become a Methodist local preacher; so I was able to offer for the Methodist ministry. Alas, when the august Dr. Scott Lidgett asked me how I knew I was called, I couldn't tell him. I just knew that I was. Thankfully, he understood, and supported me to the end of his life.

My uncle's ordination, my school boy essay, my weak association with the Congregational church, the sermon preached by a layman at the time of George V's death, my answering the need of a scout troop in a most deprived area of London, all combined to make it possible for me to hear and answer God's call to the Methodist ministry. I learnt then, and have been proving the truth of it ever since, that the things which so often seem to be obstacles are God's way of planning things out, and proving that 'All things work together for good to them that love God, who are called according to his purpose.'

Yours, as ever,
Dad

Ronald become Scoutmaster in the slums of Rotherhithe, otherwise the troop would have closed.

From: Andy Frost
To: Rob Frost
CC: Ronald Frost; Chris Frost
Subject: Call to Ministry

Dear Dad

I often feel so unsure as to why God chooses to use me, as I try to discern what is next in God's plan for my life. I had no idea what I wanted to do after university. I presumed that it would be something to do with children as my degree was in Early Childhood studies. It always amazes me how our best made plans are always changed.

What I knew for sure was that I would never work for the church and that I would never work for you, Dad. The church had always seemed to let me down and failed me in so many ways and I felt as if I owed it nothing. As for not wanting to work with you, I felt that our relationship was still vulnerable and that working together would definitely put it under too much tension.

It was while at university that I really began to get a passion for mission. The message of freedom and hope is so important in this desperate generation and I was surrounded by people who were trying to find meaning in the same hedonistic pursuits as I had earlier. Many chats about God with housemates lasted long into the night. Then my church gave me opportunities to speak at school assemblies. God had definitely planted a passion inside of me but I still presumed that this would be a spare-time hobby rather than a life calling.

When I had finished university, I was at a complete dead end. I no longer wanted to work with children (having met some!) and had no idea what was next. Meanwhile you were desperate for someone to help with the youth programmes in the office. That summer there had been some job opportunities available with other organisations but you had got involved. I am sure that your intentions were good but a twenty one year old does not want to have his father winning jobs for him. I wanted to obtain work as myself, as Andy Frost. So I got a job cooking school dinners. But cooking school dinners was not all it was cracked up to be and I knew that there was something more for me to be doing. After tense negotiations with you, Dad, I finally agreed to a temporary contract so that I could earn enough money to escape England!

The other passion in my life, that had been deepened whilst at university, was my passion for waves. With four hours a week of lectures, I was able to surf just about every day that the waves were quality enough. But I was now the proud owner of two surfboards and

'My passion for waves.'

was living in London. Whilst at university I had owned a beat-up old Renault van and had gained the nickname 'the white van man'. Almost all the student surfers knew me as I was able to cram up to ten surfers in the back of the van with surfboards. The journey to the Gower was never pleasant but the waves were always worth it. Many a journey was spent chatting about waves, creation and God.

Again, whilst at university I liked the idea of surf evangelism – it combined my favourite two hobbies! Whilst working in London, you had given me the opportunity to pioneer my own mission and Dawn Patrol quickly became reality. My initial thoughts were 10-15 surfers spending a week in Newquay, surfing and sharing. But God had different plans and by the time the summer came five churches were involved, eighty young people had enrolled and a TV crew was there to make a documentary!

I felt so out of my depth and that was exactly where God wanted me. I had to completely rely upon him for strength. For the first time in my life I felt that God was truly using me beyond my natural worth. The week was amazing – and one of the highlights was definitely seeing Chris sort out his relationship with God. I remember the night when he threw away all of his duty free cigarettes – you could almost watch the spiritual battle going on within him.

From that week I realised that I did have a gifting from God and that there was a calling upon my life for mission. Mission just seemed easy for me – I had the ability to think ahead and, whilst I would make mistakes, I saw young Christians serving God and lives being transformed! What a privilege.

My calling was further solidified through the prophetic. As a kid I always wanted to do something special for God and I always knew that he had his hand upon my life but the prophetic messages that I received helped to confirm what he had been saying to me already. The best thing about each message was that the people that gave me them did not know who my father was, yet delivered the message that they felt God was speaking to me, Andy Frost.

It was during this time that my passion for church was rekindled. It was at this time that I started preaching, believing that God could use me to bring others closer to Him.

Again there was great pressure to fit into the footsteps of both you and Grandad and there was also the problem with my clarity of speech. I tend to speak too fast, as a result of a deep felt insecurity from childhood when I had stuttered. I believe that there is a calling on me to preach but this has been much harder for me. Whenever I speak, people respond to God and his anointing is surely upon me but my speech is still not perfect and I have struggled to understand why God has not yet brought his healing touch. Yet in all of this I have to remain dependent upon Him.

So I am called to be an evangelist and a preacher. But for me there was no burning bush type experience, no calling in the night, no vision of God . . . just a gradual understanding of who I was and who God had created me to become.

Andy

From: Chris Frost
To: Rob Frost
CC: Ronald Frost; Andy Frost
Subject: Call to Ministry

Dear Dad,

One day I remember watching Andy as he was preaching
at the welcome meeting of his second Dawn Patrol mission. As I looked around the room I saw these 150 or so
faces glued to his every word. Not only had he brought
all these people together from all over the country and
from so many different walks of life but he was speaking
to them with such authority and conviction. Not for the
first time in my life I was in awe of my brother: I looked
at the man he had become and felt so insignificant in
comparison. As I knelt before the Lord at the end of that

'I was in awe of my brother.'

meeting there was a cry in my heart which resounded to the very heights of heaven: 'What is my purpose?, I look at my brother and see you have made him a fisher of men but what do you have in store for me?'

At the end of the meeting I headed for the door but was stopped in my tracks by a lady who told me that she had some prophetic words for me. I waited in anticipation as she reached out a hand and started to pray for me. Suddenly the Holy Spirit took control of me in a powerful way as the words she spoke pounded into the centre of my being: 'Christopher means Christ in you', she started, 'The fire of God is going to fall on you and just like the Olympic flame you will carry this fire to different parts of England.' I didn't fully understand what she was on about but God was making it clear to me that he had plans for my life.

That was a changing moment in my life as I started to realise God doesn't want us to live in other people's shadows but to fulfil the individual and unique purposes he has for our lives. It's still a struggle, though, living in a family which has created such big shadows. Just look at Grandpa: the Reverend Frost OBE, still a powerful preacher at the age of 82 and a real rock of faith. Or what about you, Dad: Reverend Doctor Frost, novelist, broadcaster and creator of numerous dreams and now Andy: running numerous missions and preaching everywhere.

Sometimes when I tell Christians who know our family that I'm studying broadcasting at Leeds, I get this weird look which kind of says 'Shouldn't you be at theological college?' And if the truth be told I feel inclined to agree with their disapproving eyebrows. All I want is to serve Jesus with all my life and I feel in my heart that at some time I will be called to full-time ministry. Sometimes I try and work out how student life is a stepping stone to the ministry God has called me to but at the same time I know that it's in God's will, because of all the things I'm learning about Jesus, people and life. I need to understand that all our lives are different and God needs to build different things into them in different ways.

But then I'm coming to that time when I've got to start thinking what I'm going to do after Uni and its blooming hard. God seems to have this habit of making amazing promises but not telling you how to get there. I guess just like the Israelites heading for the promised land I should stop whinging and start trusting that God will fulfil his promises. I know it would be boring if God sat us down and told us what we would be doing on what dates, just like all those guys who read their star signs.

I want to know. I just wish there was some nice Christian book called *The five steps to finding out the precise plan for your life*. Then I think of Jesus – he knew what his destiny was: Death. I guess he was probably a little more patient in fulfilling that than me. I've just got to stop thinking I'm on a tightrope wobbling towards God's promises, when in actual fact I'm walking on solid ground and as long as I'm looking to Jesus, everything is going to be cool and he'll put me where he wants me. I think part of the problem is the society we're in. Loads of my non Christian mates know what they're doing and when they're doing it and think I'm a little weird living out my faith that Jesus has a plan but I don't know exactly what it is yet. I suppose that's the road of the cross that I choose to follow.

Feels good to offload some of that.

Chris

From: Rob Frost
To: Ronald Frost
CC: Chris Frost; Andy Frost
Subject: Call to Ministry

Dear Dad, Andy and Chris,

Having read your e-mails one thing's for sure – God's call is messy!

As I've been mulling over all four of our stories, I've found it reassuring that we've all struggled to interpret what the Lord has been saying, and how Jesus has been calling us.

We all know that God doesn't only call to Christian ministry, however. This call can come to us for any kind of career or work. One of the lessons that the church has been learning over recent years has been that whether you're a bus driver or a mechanic, a surveyor or an accountant, a fast food server or a cleaner – you can be working out God's call on your life and being obedient to him. Bloom where you're planted!

I think that many Christians have also become aware that God's call can change over the years. What God is calling us to do in our twenties may be very different by the time we reach our fifties, and it may be different again by the time we're in our eighties. In the years since your retirement, Dad, you've become a full-time teacher, English tutor to Chinese students, and Christian youth worker . . . and your ministry has found a completely different direction from the years when you were a famous preacher and Central Hall minister. I know you see this new phase of ministry as part of your new calling, yet you still see yourself as a full-time Christian minister and a preacher of the gospel.

To be honest, Andy and Chris, I thought that you'd both find your main focus outside Christian ministry. I always saw you, Andy, as an eminent child psychologist . . . and Chris as the television producer that I had wanted to be at your age (and earning some decent money!). I'm thrilled that you're both following Christ's call into full-time Christian service, though, and struggling to make sense of what that really means.

As I look at the many young people who I meet and who are following a call into full-time Christian ministry like you, I am concerned that so many of them seem to feel that their call doesn't often relate to mainline church denominations. And many of those who do follow a call into ordained ministry seem to find the theological training irrelevant and the institutional church disinterested in mission. It's little wonder that some of them struggle to survive in denominational Christendom.

Time and again I find that young Christian leaders feel more at home in the less structured mentoring models of leadership development found in the house-church, rather than in the committee driven processes of institutional Christianity. I know that both of you have benefited enormously from the input of parachurch ministers and leaders with a prophetic ministry who have mentored you over recent years.

One thing is for sure, Jesus has been calling each of us into Christian ministry. That call has come to us in ways that have seemed both relevant and contemporary. And that same call is coming to thousands of others, too. I hope that our stories might encourage them to continue wrestling with that call . . . even when it's hard to interpret and even harder to obey!

Love,
Rob

3

Tough Times as a Christian

From: Rob Frost
To: Ronald Frost
CC: Andy Frost; Chris Frost
Subject: Tough Times as a Christian

Dear Dad, Andy and Chris

In these middle years of life I've come to question whether much of the super-victorious-glory-hallelujah-happy-clappy form of Christian experience which characterised my early days as a Christian wasn't, at times, just a form of escapism. I was schooled in the 'evangelical charismatic' expression of faith. Looking back, however, the years of my early discipleship lacked a good dose of harsh reality . . . and some common sense preparation for what would lie ahead.

In recent years I've had to dig deeper into the resources of faith. I've had to find a form of Christian experience which would carry me through tough times; times when every cloud wasn't covered with a superspiritual silver lining, and times when I didn't want to shout 'Praise the Lord!' Over the years I've attended 'praisey' services when no-one prayed for the world. It seemed as if the congregation was whistling in the dark; shut off from the real world: living a fantasy in a world of bless-me believing. I'm not sure that this kind of Christian experience is at all healthy.

While I consider myself to be a committed 'conservative-evangelical' I do wish that some of my mentors in the early years had prepared me better for what lay ahead. I wish that someone had told me that sometimes God would feel far away. In the heady days of my new commitment to Jesus I was so in touch with him, so united to him, so emotionally engaged with him that separation seemed impossible. The truth is, however, that there have been times when God has seemed a million miles away, unreachable, invisible and far beyond my prayers. There have been times when I've just had to cling on to his promises through a persistent act of my will.

It would have been helpful if someone had told me that I'd doubt my faith. Big questions about war, and suffering, and God's will, and the bewildering complexities that life throws up would not be sorted by a series of proof texts or a quick session of ministry. That I'd face situations when all I could do was cry out to God and ask 'why?' and find consolation nowhere except the cross.

Why didn't anyone warn me that there would be times when I'd be disillusioned? When the golden sheen of hope would disappear from life. No-one told me about the despondency I'd feel, or warned me about the violent state of the world. No one tipped me off that there would be days when I'd have to press on in a thickening fog, trusting that God would find a way ahead when I couldn't see one myself.

Back in the 'glory' days of my new found faith, why didn't anyone warn me what it was like to be spiritually low? When, no matter how good the preaching, how inspiring the worship, how warm the fellowship . . . I would remain out of sorts with myself, everyone else and even with the living God? Days when the news was so depressing that I would have to live 'the Christian plod', placing one foot before the other and 'keep on, keeping on' even when I felt like giving up?

And why didn't they warn me about the devil? That Satan's attacks would come against me at the most unexpected times and in the most unlikely places? I've had a battle on my hands that's sometimes seemed like a personal war: there is an evil one prowling around waiting to devour me whenever I step out of line!

Nowhere in my early discipleship did anyone take me to one side and let me know that sometimes God is silent. No matter how hard I might pray or how intensely I might listen, he would be nowhere to be seen. Sometimes one word of wisdom, one simple instruction, or one big arrow pointing the right way from the sky would have saved me so much hassle, so much indecision, so much struggle. Perhaps this feeling is something which comes in mid-life, when the glory glow of charismatic experience is set in the context of mountains unclimbed, ambitions unfulfilled, and revival not seen. When following Jesus seems to be about facing the harsh realities of life, fact not fiction.

Don't get me wrong: I'm still living this life: following this Risen Saviour: seeking to go where he may lead. But I find the easy Christianity of my youth less palatable now. Right now my Jesus is broken and bleeding, and he is weeping over a fallen world. And that's where I am, too. So, shall I pass the tambourine, and shall we sing the song over again? Shall we comfort ourselves with the thought that, though countless thousands suffer, we're still all right? And shall we say again 'Same place, same time, same stuff next week'. . . and pretend that nothing happens in the world between now and then?

And shall we live an infantile kind of discipleship that's so focussed on ourselves that we've nothing left

for others? Shall we busy ourselves with religion so that
there's no time to wrestle with what is happening in the
world? No. Certainly not. Let's have a faith that's rooted,
real, responsive. Amos once prophesied 'Away with the
noise of your songs! I will not listen to the music of your
harps. But let justice roll on like a river, righteousness
like a never-failing stream!' (Amos 5:23-24).

I'm genuinely thrilled when I share the charismatic
worship that so many younger Christians like you, Andy
and Chris, are discovering. I love to experience the adora-
tion you give to Jesus. I am really encouraged by the inten-
sity of your spirituality and the power of your praise. But
this can't be all. God also wants us to be real. Sometimes
we need to pass the tissues and weep with God.

God bless,
Rob

From: Ronald Frost
To: Rob Frost
CC: Andy Frost; Chris Frost
Subject: Tough Times as a Christian

Dear Robert,

I have encountered many problem periods in my life, and I know it would be helpful to others if I could let them know the kind of Christian resources that upheld me on those occasions. I have, however, encountered an unenvisaged difficulty: now that I have actually sat down to write about them much of the detail has disappeared, and I can remember very little. I am sure that I have endured many difficulties that seemed insurmountable at the time, and that I discovered the immense sufficiency of our Lord to help me cope; but trying to recollect exactly what happened many years afterwards seems practically impossible.

It is as though the precious gift of memory jettisons the worst and retains the best of what it is asked to store. I don't think that I am alone in that, for the great Quaker poet, John Greenleaf Whittier wrote, over a hundred years ago,

> That care and trial seem at last,
> Through memory's sunset air
> Like mountain ranges overpast,
> In purple distance fair.
>
> That all the jarring notes of life
> Seem blending in a psalm
> And all the angles of it strife
> Slow rounding into calm.

Consequently, it may seem strange to say that I can't really remember how I coped during the Second World War. I did not spend a single night of the six years outside of London. That meant that from September 10th 1940 to April 30th 1945, scarcely a day or night went by without my life being in danger from Hitler's bombs, doodle-bugs or V2 rockets.

I looked after a little church on the banks of the river Thames in Rotherhithe. I worked at all hours of the day and night for the Ministry of War transport, getting food supplies out of the London docks; and my home – which I rarely saw – was in Lewisham. These were three areas where it was certain that if you were not raided in one, you would be attacked in another! Yet the emotions of fear and relief, that I must have had, have quite disappeared from memory.

I do recall one terrible night, when I was on duty with the 1st Bermondsey Scout troop, (who were presented with the George Medal for their courage by King George VI). We were in the deep shelter under the Bermondsey Central Hall when we realised that the road outside had received a direct hit. The only exit was blocked with heavy, and apparently irremovable masonry. Dr. Leslie Davison, trying to keep the shelterers calm, suggested that we should sing. Those cheerful cockney men, women and children gave hearty voice to all the traditional pub songs of the time.

Then a rough dock labourer called out, 'Guv, let's 'ave "Tell me the old old story."' I knew, and everybody else knew, that this was a hymn parodied in most unwholesome circumstances, but that was not the case then. They knew that none of us might get out alive, but they wanted to sing,

> Yes, and when THAT world's glory
> Is dawning on my soul,
> Tell me the Old, Old Story,
> Christ Jesus makes thee whole.

I cannot re-live the emotions of that time of crisis, but I do not doubt that it was Christ Jesus who kept us going, and who motivated aid to achieve our ultimate deliverance. Similarly, although I cannot clearly recall how I got through other times of crisis, I am sure that I could not have done so without my faith. It is that which makes divine help so real.

I witnessed this most of all during my dear wife's long and painful illness. Her favourite hymn was, 'I know that my Redeemer lives.' It contains the line 'He lives and gives me daily breath.' With her long years of suffering with chronic bronchial asthma, she knew that what breath she did get was not just due to all the medicines and appliances that the wonderful medical people got for her. She knew that even they would be insufficient without her faith in Jesus. When, during the last twenty-five years of her life, rheumatoid arthritis added to her pain, she only seemed to become more happy and less complaining. On the Sunday night before she died she fulfilled her office as a local preacher. Propped up in her wheelchair, placed within the communion rail of the Miller Memorial church in Tottenham, she brought real joy into the worship.

She had always shared my ministry, in the great Central Halls of Stoke-on-Trent, Plymouth and Birmingham, but in her most incapacitated state, she really came into her own in Tottenham. She was invited to take over the leadership of the Thursday afternoon sisterhood, and its membership trebled during her time. All around the area of small old houses, and modern huge tower-block flats, women said to their complaining neighbours 'What are you grumbling about? You want to come and see our minister's wife on a Thursday afternoon. You come and see how she copes.' So they came, and found this breathless crippled leader, so full of fun and laughter, always smiling, always with a cheerful word for those she encountered. They didn't only come to the meetings, they found her secret, and began to share her faith.

Freda Mary Frost got through adversity because she believed that St Paul's experience could be true for her. He wrote in 2 Corinthians chapter 12, verse 7, 'There was given me a thorn in the flesh . . . three times I appealed to the Lord to remove it from me, but he said to me, 'My grace is sufficient for thee, my strength is made perfect in weakness.'

Sincerely,
Ronald

Ronald's wife Freda, holding baby Andrew.

From: Andy Frost
To: Rob Frost
CC: Ronald Frost; Chris Frost
Subject: Tough Times as a Christian

Dear Dad,

I know that in your life you have had a lot of ups and downs – times when God feels so close and the vision seems so clear and times when everything seems a bit too mundane or when life is hard.

As you know, I love to climb mountains – climbing the three peaks of Ben Nevis, Scafell and Snowdon in twenty-four hours was definitely a challenging experience. As I move on in my ministry, it is amazing how life is so similar – a series of mountaintops and valleys. When you are on the mountaintop, the view seems clear, you feel close to God and you are just so excited to be alive. The valleys on the other hand are dark places . . . often lonely, and even when you cry out to God, he can seem so distant.

I love the story of the Transfiguration and I was thinking the other week how it happened on top of a mountain – not a hill, but a mountain. It dawned on me that Jesus and his three companions must have struggled together as they ascended to the top. Yet when they finally made it and had that awesome encounter, it would have made it all worthwhile. But I wonder if, in the following weeks, months and years, the disciples longed to be back on that mountaintop and in the presence of Moses, Elijah and of course Jesus.

The moment God imparts his vision into your life, you buzz with excitement, expectancy and awe. God has chosen to use you to put his plan into action. I love those revelations. But then comes the process of turning this vision into reality – the hard work, the late nights and the waiting upon God. Sometimes I begin to doubt whether God has really spoken to me or whether I have imagined it. At the same time there is a need to continue persevering and when friends and colleagues have thrown themselves into the vision, I need to remain confident in God's promises. There are times when I wish that I had never been given the vision in the first place and that I had instead chosen a career in telesales!

These are the lonely times, closed off to the public. I cry out to God, asking for fresh revelation and confirmation. But Satan plagues me with snares and traps – fear and doubt. No longer am I on a platform basking in the glory – instead I am sat in front of a computer at midnight with stress levels rising and mugs of cold coffee surrounding me. Did I really hear God correctly?

Yet these times are desperately important if I am ever to remain humble. If life ran in a series of mountain top experiences, then they would become everyday and under-rated. If mountaintops were the norm, I would have no need to rely upon God and would start working in my own strength. But the valleys and the slow ascents are desperately hard and people never seem to realise the sweat and tears that go into any project. They just turn up and consume – little thanks is shown. I think of Elijah and his desperation. In today's world, leaders are expected to remain strong and confident – there is no allowance for weakness. This philosophy has been adopted by the church and there is no opportunity for pastors and preachers to be honest.

One of the hardest lessons that I have learnt so far has been the difference between expectation and presumption. Expectation is a vital quality in a visionary. If we do not expect God to move then everything is futile. Yet presuming God will act in a certain way is dangerous. On the first club outreach night that I had helped organise, we saw God do the most amazing things. It was like a snapshot of something in the book of Acts – God's glory fell and the gifts of the Spirit were used to bring many to faith. The following year and we were back in the same club. We were expectant but I was also presumptuous. People were making commitments but I was not satisfied with the way it was happening. I wanted God to work through the same methods as the year before. I became almost angry with God, feeling let down and betrayed. Yet by the end of the night five people had come to know him!

God cannot be shaped or boxed. He is the Creator and has complete authority. But as I try to understand him, the more I grasp the more I don't understand. If we were able to understand him more fully, the valley experiences would make more sense and we would have a clearer idea of what was happening and what our jigsaw piece was meant for. Yet as I will never understand God, neither will I ever understand his grace and the way that he picks me up in the valleys and gives me the desire to persevere.

The hardest valleys are those created by the church. I read the Bible and I glimpse what the church should be and I weep as I see a church that fights and fears; a church that is not unified, but bureaucratic, visionless, apathetic and satisfied. I see churches failing to engage with society and cocooning themselves into a false reality.

Then I see my own shortcomings – my devotion to projects and events rather than the God who birthed them in my heart; my failings as I strive for a life of righteousness and integrity that is too often engulfed in pride, lust and earthly desires. When I see how far I am from the perfection that Christ calls us to, my heart weeps. I have come to the conclusion that he who dreams much suffers much. I dream of a day when towns, cities and countries are won for Christ, when the church again has a jealousy for God's name and when I might be called 'good and faithful servant'. But until all worship, I suffer as I hunger after God and his will. I wander lonely in the valleys waiting for my God to deliver us.

Andy

From: Chris Frost
To: Rob Frost
CC: Ronald Frost; Andy Frost
Subject: Tough Times as a Christian

Hey Dad,

I sometimes look at your life in awe. As I bounce up to you with a childlike enthusiasm about the latest book I've read or the latest revelation I've had in prayer you meet me with a warming, but slightly condescending smile which says 'I'm happy for you, son, but that's old news, mate.' It's at times like this when I want to jump inside your head and suck up all the wells of knowledge that lie inside, if only to avoid learning things the hard way.

During my honeymoon period with Jesus I never used to believe in these valleys that Christians went on about. I would listen to people weepingly describe how they were in a desert time and I felt like heckling 'you wimp!' I ended up eating my words just a couple of months later.

I can remember the start of the period well. Every time I went to worship . . . nothing; no thunderbolt of the Spirit, no prophetic word and not even a softly spoken 'I love you.' I was devastated. Where had the lover gone that I knew so intimately? I scanned my last week's sin list: was there anything that could have turned him away?

Nothing . . . well nothing out of the ordinary. I was stuck in a spiritual Siberia; a place that I didn't even believe existed. It felt like hell trying to keep up a sparkling smile at extended worship sessions. My face would burn with guilt as my mates sung the chorus: 'I will dance, I will sing' for the fourth time in a row. Why wasn't I feeling it? I'd try praying but that just seemed to make me more frustrated. Evangelism was just embarrassing: it was like trying to tell people how to get water when I was dying of thirst myself.

Looking back, I learnt more in that period about perseverance and patience than anyone could ever have taught me. But where was the preparation? Why had no one sat me down and told me the truth about these times? I totally agree with you Dad: Sometimes I feel like we Christians are living in a charismatic bubble where anyone whinging or expressing hardship is lobbed out the back of the church with all the other people who have a need. It's all a bit too close for comfort; we'll stick with our smiling, blue-eyed Jesus, thank you very much, where nothing ever goes wrong.

Then I look upon the path of this life before me and I see it covered with hardship and suffering: a life that barely recognises popularity, comfort and earthly riches! I want to please the one I love and I'm promised it will be worth it, but what keeps you going on Monday mornings when the ones you trust have let you down and no one understands? Is it really worth the hurt and pain? And what about when no one seems to care or even notice, how do you know that it's not as pointless as chasing the wind?

I look at the heroes of our faith and I'm astounded how they can persevere through the toughest of times: Brother Yun being beaten to a pulp, John Wesley meeting stones and abuse, along with countless other sufferers for the gospel. And it seems that our nation will see a rise in persecution again. So what's the key to perseverance and joy in the pain?

I don't want to say that my walk has been all doom and gloom because it hasn't, but how long will it be until there are songs of lament in our worship, until the hard times are prophesied and until it is taught that blessed are those who are weak in spirit? When will we hear preaching about the Israelites in the wilderness, Ruth plodding along with Naomi or Jesus' temptation in the desert? I'm the first one up for a super-spiritual celebration in the very heights of heaven but we can't get lost there; we've got to bring that reality down to the earth that needs it so desperately.

All my love,
Chris

From: Rob Frost
To: Ronald Frost
CC: Andy Frost; Chris Frost
Subject: Tough Times as a Christian

Dear Dad, Andy and Chris,

I was fascinated by your stories of the Blitz, Dad. I can't help but think that there was a much greater sense of stoicism in your era than in the current generation. Maybe your war-time experiences toughened you so that your tolerance threshold of hard times is higher than that of those who've only lived through a more peaceful era. I well remember the suffering that Mum went through in the last years of her life. There were times when she really did struggle, but I saw for myself how her faith enriched her life – and how her simple trust in Jesus enabled her to seek ways of redeeming her suffering.

You have demonstrated that faith can weather some pretty dreadful storms, and your example of stickability is something which many of us need to discover for ourselves. Many people who've lost their faith because of the way that life has turned out need to discover again your experience of Gethsemane, Golgotha and the Empty Tomb.

I strongly relate to your mountaintops and valleys experience, Andy. Often the hardest times for me are in the preparation phase for a big project or mission, when the vision can be obscured by the sheer weight of responsibility. Often the paperwork and the intense pressures of budgeting and fund-raising really get me down. Then, when the project is over and the adrenaline rush is gone, I can be left with a feeling of exhaustion and failure . . . even when everyone says how blessed they've been!

I was glad you mentioned Brother Yun, Chris. The morning that he was the guest on my Premier Radio show made a profound impact on both of us. You were helping me at the studio that morning, and as he told his story of torture and persecution I could sense how moved you were. Later, I remember looking out of the studio window into the reception area as you were showing him out, and seeing you kneeling there as Brother Yun prayed over you. When, later, I asked you what was happening, you simply said 'I want some of what that man has got!'

I think it's clear that all of us believe in being real in our faith. Christianity isn't about some kind of warm emotional glow which is an escape from the hardships and suffering of life, but a real source of strength and grace which can help us to face the tough times, deal with them and even redeem them. We've all discovered

Rob hosts the Sunday Breakfast Show at Premier Radio.

that the Christian life isn't a bed of roses. As you, Andy and Chris, have both admitted, it's about valleys as well as about mountaintops, and it's about perseverance and joy . . . even in pain.

Maybe some of those who look at us and who think we have an easier life than they, will get a different perspective from this correspondence. I'm convinced that when the going gets tough . . . the tough must get going after God.

Rob

4

Spiritual Highs

From: Rob Frost
To: Ronald Frost
CC: Andy Frost; Chris Frost
Subject: Spiritual Highs

Dear Dad, Andy and Chris,

We share a common dream. All of us yearn to see a true revival here in the United Kingdom. I know, Dad, that you've ministered for a lifetime here in the United Kingdom, and longed to see a Holy Spirit revival. You've told me about the great Welsh revival, and you've always been fascinated by what happened through John and Charles Wesley in the eighteenth century. But you've never seen a revival for yourself. I know that both Andy and Chris also long to see revival. But what do we all mean? And what are we all really hoping for?

A couple of years ago there was a new tourism fad in the United States. Tens of thousands of Americans were flocking to a Florida beach resort called Pensacola for what many locals call some 'Pensacola Pentecostal fizz'.

Talk to any hotel receptionist, taxi driver or airport worker and ask what their town is most famous for and they'll tell you: 'The Brownsville Revival'. When I told my friends that I was going to see it for myself I met a diverse range of reactions.

'The wacky end of Christian experience' said one.

'The Holy Spirit's left but no-one told the people' said another.

'They're gonna get you big-time . . . even in the car park' warned a fellow minister.

'It'll change your life forever' my Pentecostal friend beamed.

On the morning that I first visited Brownsville Assemblies of God church where the revival was focussed, there was a massive queue of people in the car park waiting to get in. That may not seem surprising . . . apart from the fact that the service didn't start for another seven hours! In the intense Florida heat the cola and ice cream sales team were certainly doing brisk business.

I didn't have to queue, however. I claimed my VIP status under the category of 'foreign church leader' and was privileged to get a back door pass and a reserved seat near the front row. (It's not what you know but who you know . . . even in a revival!)

Quite frankly, I was disappointed. The worship was deafening, the preaching shallow, the Mexican-wave style liturgy weak. Yet I don't doubt that thousands of people were blessed that night . . . and as hundreds ran toward the altar in broken repentance I felt something of a pagan as I remained firmly in my seat. I don't doubt that there has been a powerful move of the Holy Spirit in Pensacola over recent years. More than 144,000 people have given their lives to Christ and thousands more have experienced personal renewal in powerful ways.

But the revival hasn't only touched the Assemblies of God church in Brownsville. A Methodist Church out in the suburbs of Pensacola at Pine Forest has also been transformed by this move of the Holy Spirit.

The young people from their youth group attended the Brownsville Revival Meetings first, but soon they dragged their parents along. Finally, the Reverend Perry Dalton, the United Methodist Pastor, went downtown to see what all the fuss was about. His own ministry was changed and renewed that night, and he began to call the local Methodist congregation to fasting and prayer. The Methodist folk were touched by the Holy Spirit, and it led to a painful and powerful time of confession, repentance and forgiveness. Families were brought together, marriages healed, parents and children reunited, and many deep pastoral situations brought out into the open to be ministered to through prayer and counselling.

It wasn't all good news, though. About one third of the local congregation resigned their membership in protest at the change of emphasis and direction of their local church. As they left, however, many others, particularly on the fringes of church life, came to take their place.

I called in at the church late one Saturday evening to check on the order of service, as I was preaching there next morning. The lights in the sanctuary were all blazing, and I found that there were lots of people praying inside. I crept in and found the minister. He explained that the congregation was already gathering to pray throughout the night for the worship the next morning.

When I arrived back at the church the next morning to preach, I was really moved to see that the intercession group was still there, and still praying! When the service began I was amazed to discover that it was quite a traditional form of worship. There was a choir, robed altar boys and a fairly liturgical format.

When I announced the first hymn and people stood to sing, the sense of the Holy Spirit was so overwhelming that it was almost tangible. By the second verse, four people were kneeling at the altar rail in floods of tears, wanting to confess their sins and to get right with God.

By the time I started to preach about half of the packed congregation was already at the altar rail, and the prayer team was at work among them. I turned to the pastor and asked if I should still preach. He urged me to do so, and as I continued yet more of the congregation came forward in repentance. By the end of the service the sense of God's presence was so strong that hardly anyone was left in the pew, and even I was prostrate at the altar. While there were many aspects of this revival that I personally struggled with, and certain phenomena which bothered me, I was left with one overwhelming response. If the Holy Spirit can move in renewing a fairly traditional United Methodist church in suburban Florida . . . he can do it anywhere!

Perhaps we have sanitised the Holy Spirit and made him too safe. Perhaps the dry form of Christianity to be found in many of our churches needs the refreshing power of the Holy Spirit to shake us up and to remind us whose church it really is. There was certainly nothing safe about that first Pentecost described in the Acts of the Apostles. Luke described his arrival as the blowing of a violent wind which filled the whole house. Large fiery flames rushed through the house, divided, and rested on the individual disciples. They began to talk in strange languages. Scary stuff.

Having experienced Pine Forest United Methodist church for myself . . . these things don't seem as impossible as once they did. If God could do it in a mainline traditional American church . . . he could do it for many of our institutional churches here in Britain. But why would he do it? Why would he send a fresh anointing of the Holy Spirit? Why would he 'zap' us in fresh ways? I don't believe he'd do it just to give us a warm glow inside or to get us dancing in the aisles.

No. The Bible makes it clear why God sends the Holy Spirit. Time and again when God sends the Holy Spirit, he sends him for mission. In John 20 (vv 21–22) Jesus tells his disciples that, as the Father has sent him . . . so he is sending them. Immediately he breathes on them and tells them to receive the Holy Spirit. He's given them power to fulfil the great Commission.

I've seen a tangible expression of revival for myself, and it really blew me away. It's encouraged me to look for more, and I've been deeply challenged by the sense of expectation which you all have that the Holy Spirit will move in power again . . . and that he will do a new thing among us. And I'm sure that the key to it is prayer.

God bless,
Rob

From: Ronald Frost
To: Rob Frost
CC: Andy Frost; Chris Frost
Subject: Spiritual Highs

Dear Robert,

On the last night of every Boys' Brigade camp a special
hymn is sung, which begins,

> We thank Thee, O our Father,
> Before the memories fade,
> For all Thy love around us . . .

Therefore, although I have received so many blessings in
life, the one that I particularly want to mention before it
fades is quite recent. It happened in fact when I was privileged to go on a pilgrimage to Israel in the summer of 2002.

One day we were taken to the traditional site of the
Upper Room. That was a cold area, with a flagstoned
floor, and windows high up in tall bare walls. It had no
atmosphere to thrill a visitor, no indication that this was
the place where Jesus had eaten the Last Supper with his
disciples, where he had met them on the evening of
Resurrection day, and where the Holy Spirit descended
with such power at Pentecost seven weeks later.

As we left, our tour guide said, 'Now I would like to
take you to St. Mark's church, which is not on the official
route.' He took us to a Syrian Orthodox church, and
directed us to an ancient stone in the interior wall of the
building. The words on it were in an Aramaic script
used in the fifth century AD. Translated, it read 'This is
the house of St. Mark, the first church in Christianity,
where the Last Supper was performed, and where the
Holy Spirit came down upon the Apostles at Pentecost.'

This stone with its inscription had been covered with plaster and paint for centuries, but was discovered when the place was being renovated in September 1940. It had apparently been put there in the fifth century.

This then, it was claimed was the true Upper Room. I had listened to all this commentary, and settled myself in a pew by the font, when it was suggested that in such a sacred place we ought to pray. Someone did pray, and so did someone else, then a voice broke into song and others joined in. Then there were more prayers and people quoted Scripture. Sometimes more than one person was speaking at the same time. Some people rose to their feet and held up their arms, others knelt down. Strange noises began to emerge, which I presumed were speaking in tongues – a phenomenon with which, in my more prosaic liturgy, I am not familiar.

I don't know how long the tour guide had allowed for this unscheduled stop, but he was no longer in command. Everyone, so it seemed to me, was just overtaken by the Holy Spirit. The exuberance of modern Pentecostal style worship is foreign to me, but as I sat quietly in my corner; my eyes closed, I had the reassurance of God's presence in my own life – rather like John Wesley feeling his heart 'strangely warmed.'

Then it struck me that all the people speaking were not of one kind. Some of the prayers, quietly uttered, were from the Book of Common prayer, and when a voice struck up, 'Here O my Lord I see Thee face to face,' voices that had previously been singing more up-to-date melodies joined in. In short, this was something that could not have been organised, and it included every facet of Christian worship. There was no sense of one mode being more acceptable than another. There was just a wonderful sense of togetherness.

From my quiet corner, I did wonder how it would all end, but it did. Ultimately things grew quieter, I opened my eyes to see people returning to their seats, or rising from their knees. Then I saw a young man prone on the floor, experiencing what I think is called being 'slain in the Spirit.' It was my grandson, Christopher.

This was no exhibitionism, but part of the manifestation of the outpouring of the Holy Spirit that we had all experienced, although maybe in diverse ways. I needed no further proof that this was the home of the mother of John Mark, where such a movement of divine power had been felt on the day of pentecost soon after the ascension of Jesus.

I was even more convinced of the validity of what happened on that day when on the last day of the tour, when the rest of us were looking forward to returning to our homes, my grandson stayed behind to give a month of his university vacation to organising sports activities for the poorest Arab children in Jerusalem, in the hope that something of Christ's love would reach them, through what he was doing.

It was in Saint Mark's church on Mount Zion that I had a mountain top experience of God's presence.

As ever,
Dad

Ronald, Rob and Chris on the Sea of Gallilee.

From: Andy Frost
To: Rob Frost
CC: Ronald Frost; Chris Frost
Subject: Spiritual Highs

Dear Dad,

The highs in my life have to include the excitement of travelling down to the beach with friends in a crowded car with the expectant chatter reaching fever pitch. The mental preparation for wave conditions reported as four foot and glassy – perfect. The smell of the wax as you rub down your board, desperate to get into the water and the cool refreshing shudder as you duck dive the first wave. Then wait for the prime wave as the sun warms your face and the thrill of gliding across the face of a wave or pulling a new trick – immense!

The highs would also have to include the perfect setting with the camp fire crackling away as I lie back and gaze at the stars. The barbecue food is slowly digested and the cold beer sits in my hand. The deep conversation as close friends share intimate thoughts. The full understanding of friendship as thoughts of work, pensions and modern day life fade into insignificance.

Maybe the greatest high of all is the nervous expectancy as you reach the front and turn to face the crowd, completely out of your comfort zone. Then slowly watching the anxious face turn to laughter with the first illustration. The first point then challenges to the core. The guitar strums up and the appeal is made and people choose to follow him . . . God has used me to bring people to him – surely the greatest high?

Life does have some great highs – my competitive personality means that I want to get as much out of life as possible. I want to achieve all I can, and do so much.

You probably remember the disappointment as I kept failing my driving test. First of all braking too soon and the next for braking too late . . . I remember how good it felt when I finally passed my driving test – fifth time! I think it must have been a high in your life, too, as we went for a pub lunch and you knew that you would never have to help me reverse park again.

Relationships are key in those highs. If you have no one to share a great piece of news with, no-one with whom to celebrate success, then the high can quickly become a low. So many people invest all they have in their passion for fame or fortune, but when they finally reach their destination, they have no one to share it with.

Being in ministry is also a real high. Seeing people come to know Jesus is awesome. I always find it quite bizarre when people see me as a role model and look up to me, when people take my advice seriously and want

'Relationships are key in those highs.'

me to pray for them. It is such a privilege to share in people's lives and help them find their calling. One of the greatest things was seeing Chris transformed by God. Those are the kind of highs in ministry that are so exciting!

Yet these are not the ultimate highs of my life – the true highs have not come at the front of a church or at a big event. The ultimate highs come on idle Tuesday afternoons, when nothing exciting is in the diary but when I have met with God. When I speak face to face with the all powerful God, the Alpha and the Omega, the Creator of the universe, the King of all kings and the Lord of all Lords – now that is an ultimate high!

This is the most amazing high that I have ever known. I, just another person in an overpopulated world, am loved by God. And the more I think about it, the more my head hurts; the more that I try to explain it, the more my mind boggles; and yet the more my heart rejoices. Thank you, God. The greatest thing I know is that the Lord God loves me and cares for me. It sounds so cheesy but the truth pierces my heart. No matter how low I can feel and how lonely I can be, the Lord God so loved me that he sent his only Son to die for me.

Whenever it all looks bleak, he is my hope. Whenever it all appears too much, he is there by my side. Whenever I feel weak, he is my strength. I love that passage in 2 Corinthians 5 when Paul describes us as being like jars of clay – wasting away on the outside yet with this treasure within us. Much of the time that is exactly how I feel. I am renewed internally by the Father who loves me – the all-powerful, all-knowing, all-present lover of my soul. Yet on the outside I am wasting away.

I love the story of Moses. He hungers after God and is always desiring more. Tommy Tenney describes him as a Godchaser – someone that seeks God's face. He meets

God in a burning bush but is not satisfied – he desires more. Moses then ascends the mountain that has a layer of smoke around its peak and thunder and lightning. All the other Israelites refuse to go up the mountain but he desires God. Even then he is not satisfied and desires to see God in all his glory. Although Moses saw great things happen, though he saw the Red Sea part and the Israelites set free; though he saw manna fall from heaven and great armies defeated; speaking face to face with God must have been the greatest high. That intimacy with the Father is spectacular!

I, too, desire God – I passionately want more. As I walk around the local park, talking with God, that is better than surfing any wave. As I open my heart to experience God's love day by day, that is better than any human love. As I am broken, moulded and shaped, it is so great to know that being his is so much more important than doing anything for him. His grace is something I could never earn.

Off for another ultimate high with the Father,

Andy

From: Chris Frost
To: Rob Frost
CC: Ronald Frost; Andy Frost
Subject: Spiritual Highs

Dear Dad,

Do you remember when we went on 'The Big One' at
Blackpool pleasure beach? The cart would creak up the
steep track slowly but surely and then plummet down to
the blurry floor beneath. I think my early Christian
journey has definitely been like a bit of a spiritual roller-
coaster; up one minute and down the next but as truth
has slowly started to bear fruit in my life, the roller-
coaster tracks seem to have smoothed out a bit.
Sometimes the adventure seems a little less reckless and
exciting now but maturity brings a blessing too.

'You've got to experience the lows to enjoy the highs.'

I think my high definitely starts with a low but as that Tom Cruise blockbuster, *Minority Report* so profoundly stated 'You've got to experience the lows to enjoy the highs.' I don't know when it started, or even how it happened: I guess it was probably a gradual thing but as I go to different churches I can see so many others in the same predicament. I think John the Divine puts it best in the book of Revelation when Jesus is addressing the church in Ephesus; 'I see your good works . . . but I hold this against you; you have forgotten your first love.'

I was pushing along in my first term at Leeds university and everything was becoming a bit of a drag. I was trapped in a prison of works. I would spend any free moment reading the Bible, praying or telling people about Jesus, desperately seeking to meet God's approval. There was an aggressive urgency in me about doing everything that I possibly could. Then at the same time I was constantly aware of how sinful I was; I would implement stricter and stricter boundaries upon myself to such an extent that I'd often avoid conversation. I became so judgemental of other Christians and was offended at their supposed little effort, but in actual fact I was struggling more than any of them.

The guy's name was Bob, although I guess that doesn't really matter but as soon as he started speaking, I knew this was going to be a special time. Over the next few days my life took a big U-turn, so much of what I held to was being flipped on its head. I was released from my prison and bang! I had a head-on collision with grace. I was in and out of hysterics in the presence of God for about a week. It was absolutely amazing: I felt like a child embracing my heavenly Dad and I realised that nothing I could do would make him love me more or less. It was a pleasure to serve him again and I took delight in studying his word. Oh to be free!

When you asked me to write this letter there have been so many highs: leading loads of youngsters to Christ, meeting my girlfriend Jo and seeing dramatic outbursts of God's power but deep down I know that I would be in a much darker place if I hadn't grasped grace when I did. I know that I'd still be relying on my own strength to see things happen. I acknowledge that it's my understanding of grace that has allowed me to see Jesus move in the ways I have and I know that it's grace which has kept me going in the hard times.

Love,
Chris

'Meeting my girlfriend Jo.'

From: Rob Frost
To: Ronald Frost
CC: Andy Frost; Chris Frost
Subject: Spiritual Highs

Dear Dad, Andy and Chris,

I was glad that the experience in St Mark's church in
Jerusalem was so powerful for you, Dad. It was certainly memorable for me, too. The sense of connection
with the past in such an ancient building, having you
and Chris with me . . . and seeing the Holy Spirit fall
with such power made that simple prayer meeting very
special.

I have struggled with some of the phenomena of
Pentecostalism over the years, and I well remember
praying when I was at Bible college 'Lord, I would like
the Holy Spirit, but I'd rather not have the Pentecostal
baggage which goes with him!' I really struggled with
the noisy exuberance of Pentecostal prayer meetings,
speaking in tongues and the unstructured 'anything
goes' mentality of worship in the Spirit. God gave me
the Holy Spirit then, and over the years I've been learning to appreciate some of the things that once turned me
off.

I've seen God work powerfully in your life, Chris, and
it's evident that you've found a rich awareness of grace.
Your brand of Christian experience is thoroughly
Pentecostal . . . and while I've been a bit of a closet
charismatic, you really go for it! You've been teaching
me to let go of some of my British reserve and to enter
into more of the fullness that God has for me.

There is so much which God has to give us, so many
gifts, so much fruit . . . that we should never stop asking
for more. In recent months God has been teaching me

that our experience of the Holy Spirit should always be present tense. We're not like camels, going through the desert until we can drink at the next oasis. The Holy Spirit is a spring of living water, always flowing through our lives, if only we'll allow him.

But that's not all. I've been learning from you too, Andy. You demonstrate in your everyday life that spirituality is not confined to religious settings. Your spirituality is experienced in riding the surf, or in rich conversation with close friends, or in good barbecued food . . . as well as in worship or in seeing men and women born again. You live with a deep awareness that God infuses the whole of life with his Spirit, it's just a matter of recognising his presence . . . and of being open to him in any setting. I want more of that, too.

God is very gracious. In these mid-years of life I can honestly say that I'm learning from my sons as well as my dad. God has so much more for each of us wherever we are on life's journey . . . let's press on to inherit the land.

Thanks,
Rob

5

A Vision for Mission

From: Rob Frost
To: Ronald Frost
CC: Andy Frost; Chris Frost
Subject: A Vision for Mission

Dear Dad, Andy and Chris,

I guess our family has always been up for innovation when it comes to evangelism. As I look back across the years I vividly remember how you have proclaimed the gospel, Dad. I used to stand in Birmingham Bull Ring open air market and watch as you put a Christian perspective on the week's news, sometimes with hundreds of onlookers cheering and barracking you! I remember your work among hippies, when you ran the Cellar Club in Birmingham, and were way ahead of your time as you encountered serious drug abuse in Birmingham city centre in the 60s. And your great evangelistic productions, when you used drama and music in worship whilst others considered it heretical. Perhaps you remember how we built a 'tropical island' including palm trees and a beach to illustrate the 'Story of Christmas Island' for a carol service.

Just over thirty years ago you encouraged me to organise my first beach mission at Newquay, in Cornwall. It was a nerve-racking time, as about a hundred of my Christian friends descended on that small Cornish holiday resort. At one point Ishmael and I nearly got arrested for a breach of the peace, after we drew a crowd of over two hundred young holidaymakers for an open-air meeting at 11:30 pm one night! The police were not amused.

All those years ago I realised how impossible the task of evangelism in such a secular setting was. Preaching seemed a turn-off, and testimony didn't seem to draw people . . . and much of our singing left a lot to be desired! In sheer desperation we began to use drama . . . simple gospel sketches, which were loud, funny, colourful and even bizarre. And, to our great delight, people started to gather. Sometimes sixty or more holidaymakers would stop to stare at our antics . . . and, hopefully, get the message. At that time drama in church was practically unknown, and I remember the stir that these simple experiments caused. Some of my peers felt that unless the message was preached, it couldn't be authentic.

Over the thirty years since my mission in Newquay this has all changed. There are now several professional Christian theatre and dance companies, several year long courses that specialise in the church's use of the creative arts, and lots of churches who use drama as part of their ongoing outreach programmes and worship services. Actor Nigel Forde once defined the role of drama in church life. 'Prophetic theatre is theatre which clarifies the word of God at a particular time; Evangelistic theatre is that which clarifies the gospel in particular; Didactic theatre clarifies the teaching of the Bible and Entertaining Theatre is based on the nature of humankind and creation.' I've come to believe that the arts are a crucial means of communicating Christian truth today.

Over past centuries the church used drama as an integral part of its communication. Yet today drama and the creative arts are often relegated to special guest services or entrusted to those with little skill or expertise. The church must put drama back centre-stage. The primary role of drama in proclamation is not to hammer home the message but to grab the audience's attention, to entertain, to tell stories, to raise questions, to hold up a mirror to human experience and to question people's presuppositions, so that the preacher has a listening audience waiting to make a connection. Drama is at its most useful when the viewers, empathising with the characters, recognise some situation or aspect of their lives and become riveted by the plot and open to the message.

When I visited you, Andy and Chris, with around a hundred of your mates working on mission in Newquay, where I had worked around thirty years ago, I was overwhelmed by emotion. You were doing a surf mission, and trying to reach young people who have found connection with nature, but not with Jesus Christ. Both missions, thirty years apart, share the same simple commission: to communicate the faith to the hundreds of holidaymakers with a few minutes to spare.

I'm thrilled that you are both engaged in front-line evangelism and that you, too, are using drama as part of your outreach, particularly in your open air witness in Newquay town centre. Street theatre has certainly come a long way since we first used it. Your mime, sketches and dance teams pull in a much younger crowd than my material would! Drama, both inside and outside the church, doesn't seem anywhere near as strange or raw as it did thirty years ago.

I'm really encouraged that you are pushing back the boundaries of evangelism for a new generation. Many of the things that you are doing seem as strange to me as my evangelistic techniques must have seemed to the church leaders of my youth. I watched as you co-ordinated a skateboard competition involving scores of local teenagers. I saw your team leading prayers over the intercom at a major national surfing event. I walked around your contemporary art exhibition in the town centre. I saw your surfing videos in the marquee on the beach at night. I heard the testimonies of what happened in your night-club outreach, and spoke to team members who had been praying for people on the street.

Many of these forms of outreach seem strange to me. My open air meetings, kids' clubs and film nights in the church hall seem very tame by comparison! But as I stood on the promenade and watched your teams at work on the three beaches I was moved to tears. For there, on the same sand, a generation ago we were communicating the same message in a very different culture.

'Both missions, thirty years apart, share the same commission.'

And so the work goes on. Your new and rising generation of evangelists is moving into place. It will be exciting to see what other new ways of communicating the
message and of making the gospel understandable you
all come up with next!

One thing's for sure, the use of contemporary media
in evangelism is not religious entertainment or compromise with the world . . . just effective communication.
The language of film, music, drama, poetry, art and
dance are the vernacular of the rising generation, and
we must learn how to speak it, and speak it fluently.

When I was on mission in Newquay thirty years ago, a
very old evangelist called Herbert Silverwood came to
support us. He was a real encouragement. Even though
he was in his eighties he travelled down on the coach,
offered to sleep on the floor, and joined us in our hectic
daily round of outreach meetings. One evening I watched
as he stood on a soap-box on the promenade and drew a
crowd of over two hundred people with his simple routine of Yorkshire banter. But he ended with an evangelistic appeal, and there was a queue of people waiting to
take a John's Gospel from him at the end of his talk.

Herbert had been a radical evangelist for well over
thirty years before I got started . . . he was telling jokes
and simple testimonies in the great heyday of the British
summer holiday; an era of end of the pier shows, brass
bands and candy floss. Herbert gave me one piece of
advice as he watched what we were doing. 'It's all great'
he said 'but just make sure you lift Jesus high. Because if
you do, many will be drawn to him!' I'm so thrilled to
see what you're doing, and I know that Herbert's advice
is as relevant for you as it was for me.

God bless,
Rob

From: Ronald Frost
To: Rob Frost
CC: Andy Frost; Chris Frost
Subject: A Vision for Mission

Dear Robert,

When the Methodist church first released you from an ordinary circuit appointment, I think they gave you the grand title of 'Connexional Evangelist'. I don't know if that is still the case, because in the meantime, Easter People has become both international and interdenominational. Nevertheless, when I knew that your ministry was taking you into the realm of evangelism, I (and I daresay your dear mother in glory), was delighted, for although Methodist ministers are expected to fill many different roles, none brings us nearer to John Wesley than, as Paul wrote to Timothy, 'doing the work of an evangelist.'

Having spent most of my own ministry in the superintendency of our large Central Halls in Stoke on Trent, Plymouth, Birmingham and North London, I have been expected to act as priest, prophet, pastor, preacher, politician, accountant, bus and taxi driver, caretaker and much else, but no part of the work has seemed more important to me than that of being an evangelist. I have had to remind myself sometimes that the only reason why Central Halls were invented was to head up missions in the heart of our big cities. If we didn't do mission, there was no reason for our existence. Indeed, their founder – Hugh Price Hughes – said that they were to be, 'Open-air meetings with the roof on.'

So what is evangelism? What is mission? My simple definition is 'Trying to persuade people to become Christians who would not otherwise become

Christians.' I have mentioned elsewhere that my roots are in the London City Mission, an organisation set up in the nineteenth century to persuade people in the poorer parts of that great city to accept Jesus Christ as their Saviour. Of course they did some social caring work, but that was not the main thrust of their activity; indeed they did not have the resources to do much more than pay their missionaries and maintain a few buildings.

By any contacts that they could make, the personnel of the London City Mission were to get people converted. They knew that the greatest evils in the life of any family were alcohol and gambling, but that if any member of the family was to surrender their life to Jesus, then those evils would be conquered. This would lead to more stable employment and reduce the need for hand outs and accommodation units.

Of course, in Methodism's Central Missions much social caring has been done, and one cannot pay high enough tribute to the Wesley deaconesses who were responsible for most of it. I am, however, constantly reminded of the Wesley dictum, 'Go not to those who need you, but to those who need you most.' By which he meant, not just to those in material need, but those whose lives were impoverished because they did not know the joy of sins forgiven, and the power of the Holy Spirit constantly to conquer temptation.

Broadly speaking, I think there are four ways of evangelising, but I would be interested to know if any of them are now considered obsolete, or replaceable by other ideas.

The first is through the normal contacts of life. Without embarrassing those who one meets to the extent of cramming religion down their throats, Christians should always be prepared to say a good word for the Lord. Opportunities to do that only come if our friends, acquaintances, business contacts and the rest see some-thing different in our lives because we do not live them in our own strength.

The simplest way of preventing others from believing in Jesus is for someone who professes faith to live a dis-honest, deceitful, bad-tempered, underhand, unkind, unforgiving or unloving life. Jesus said, 'By their fruits ye shall know them.' Those who don't show the fruits of the Christian life-style will not progress far as evangel-ists.

The second way of evangelising that I have pursued is by organising something that will bring people together, where the Christian faith can be proclaimed and taught. My particular involvement has been among boys, and through them their families.

During the Second World War when most men were away from home in the forces, I was seconded to the Ministry of War Transport. This meant that I had to live and work in the constantly bombed area of the London docks. When I saw children being brought back home from their places of evacuation, with very limited school facilities, I restarted the 18th Bermondsey Scout Troop, and found that I had a facility for gaining the confidence of the boys by entering into a variety of exciting and worthwhile activities with them and in that context of talking to them, sometimes as a group and sometimes more individually, about Jesus.

The fact that I was made one of the chaplains at the world jamboree, held in Sutton Park in the 1950s, seems to indicate that others perceived that I had that gift as well. For a quarter of a century after that, I served as a training commissioner attempting to pass on my meth-ods to future leaders in the movement.

Scout troops and Boys' Brigade companies have been in friendly rivalry for almost a hundred years, so it was quite a shock, when, in 1987, the 10th London Boys' Brigade Company that had met at the Archway Central Hall for over seventy years suddenly found itself leaderless. I could see no way of solving the problem other than to go to Felden Lodge and get myself trained as its captain.

From then and until the present time, I have been able not only to enter into squad drill, bugle bands, basket ball competitions, football games, figure marching competitions and the rest, but have also found an environment in which it has been possible to show the difference that trusting Jesus can make in a young man's life. There are few experiences more wonderful than sitting with two or three older teenagers round the dying embers of a camp fire and looking up at the stars, finding oneself trying to answer their questions about space, creation, the meaning of life, eternity, God and Jesus.

The camp for deprived kids at Rowney Green.

Many times in sixty years that has led to Christian commitment.

Nor is this method of evangelism confined only to boys. For the twelve years that I was in Birmingham we took thirty boys and girls each week of the school summer holidays to the mission's country grounds at Rowney Green, and no year passed without several of the campers surrendering their lives to Jesus.

The third way that I have tried to evangelise has been through the Sunday services of the church. I regret the passing of the evening service as being the best attended of the day. The morning service, I felt, could be formal and concentrate upon the worship of God. The evening service, however, I thought should be used to attract those who were not habitual church goers. I therefore tried to make the services meaningful to different groups of people, inviting various sections of the community to come and by wide publicity persuading non-churchgoers to attend. I hoped that when they came they would find a warm welcome, a happy relaxed atmosphere, good music, joyous singing and a gospel message that would help them to see that it was important to realise that Jesus was the Saviour of the world and should become their personal Saviour.

We had services for footballers, cricketers, bowling clubs, golf enthusiasts, anglers, firemen, lorry drivers, gardeners, actors and many more groups. Sometimes we spent a lot of time visiting a specific area of the city, and would then have a special service for all the people living in that neighbourhood. Sometimes we cleared all the chairs out of the ground floor of the Hall and having turned it into an arena, would get young people to perform different scenes around a theme that would end with a Christian challenge.

One particular evening in Birmingham stands out in my mind. Scores of young people had made tableaux demonstrating events with Christian significance during the twentieth century. I had prayed that some of them, because of their involvement, would respond to the appeal that I made at the end, but none of them did. There was a response, however; four men came forward. They were men of very different types; a local government officer, a teddy boy – complete with crew cut, leather suit and chains, a man recently released from prison, who was seeking confidence to go back to his wife and young family, and a school caretaker. All of them ultimately became fine Christians and were stalwart members of the church.

My fourth way of evangelism, which I dreaded but never shirked, was open air preaching. I was schooled in it in the back streets of Lower Sydenham where the

Ronald created tableaux to illustrate sermons in the Central Hall in Birmingham.

London City Mission used to hold open air services on a Sunday night. I tried it in Chipping Norton, gathering young people on the church steps opposite the bus stop, where we had a captive audience – until the bus for Oxford came, and we lost our congregation at one swoop!

I revelled in it at Burslem Wakes week where, in order to attract a crowd, Sister Barbara Facey bribed the owner of the coconut shy to give her two coconuts, so that she could attract other listeners by appearing to be an ordinary fair goer.

On summer Sunday evenings, we had an open-air service every week on Plymouth Hoe, where the Mayflower Steps and the place from which criminals were deported to Australia provided good opportunities to talk about Christian devotion and sinners' repentance.

Birmingham, however, gave a great opportunity. I was told that I could not accept the appointment unless

Ronald holding an open air meeting at Sowerby Bridge in 1950.

I agreed to preach every Friday lunchtime on the Bull Ring. This was a rather strange condition, seeing that I was 'pulled out', as we Methodists say and told by the Conference that I had to leave Plymouth and go to the second city, with no option to refuse. It was a requirement that I gladly accepted, although it was a terrifying experience. Hundreds of people milled around the Bull Ring all the time. Each week when I first got up on the stand I would think 'Won't I look foolish if no one comes to listen.' Later when the crowds began to gather, I used to think, 'I wish there was no one here, I can't answer their questions.'

My dear wife, of course, was my constant inspiration. There were very few Fridays in those twelve years that I did not keep the appointment, and on most of those occasions she was there too. She would appear to be just an ordinary shopper with her carrier bags, and if my opening address was not attracting passers-by to listen, would set me up with the first question.

There was nothing that got a crowd more easily than for there to be an argument between the man on the stand and someone in the crowd. The greatest crowd that I ever got was on the day after the I.R.A. bombed the public houses in the city centre. People wanted to know how Christ could save the world if two branches of his followers, the Catholics and the Protestants, couldn't agree among themselves. Others wanted to know how anyone acting with the approval of any part of the Christian church could cause such indiscriminate death and destruction in an unsuspecting area. It was embarrassing to try and own the deficiencies of the church, as being contrary to the teachings of its founder. This was especially difficult in Birmingham, where there were such excellent relationships between all the Christian denominations.

There were, of course, other days when the listeners were very sparse. The meeting was always held, even if only a dozen of us had to resort to the awning around Woolworths to get out of the rain or snow. Even in the worst weather my faithful supporters would come. There were only two or three from the Mission, I am bound to say, but always present, with one or two others, were a farmer who was a member of the Strict Brethren, a man from the Secularist Society who was opposed to all religion, and a young woman who claimed to be a witch.

They were as loyal as any indoor church congregation and on the unforgettable day when I was heckled by a young Moslem, all my regulars, who usually opposed me, swung round on my side. That was the other occasion when we drew a really mammoth crowd. It was in 1976 and there was no mosque in Birmingham then, and I got support from all sides. Courageously the young man expressed his own point of view, and tried to counter all the statements that I made. The applause and congratulations that I got from all sides clearly indicated that even if people didn't go to church, they valued the Christian ethic.

Defeated in argument, the young man finished with a loud acclamation, that has become more true than we could ever have envisaged at that time. He said 'You may win today, but we have already captured southern Europe, we are well established in France, and by the end of the century Britain will be Moslem.'

The next day he came to see me in my office and apologised. I told him that he had nothing for which to apologise; we had had a fair debate, and I admired his courage in bearing his witness in such a hostile environment. 'No,' he said, 'I haven't come to apologise for that, but for the fact that in our religion we are taught always to show respect to our elders, and I felt that I failed in that by the way that I attacked you yesterday.' His courtesy was indeed a great credit to his faith. How I wished that I could have brought him to Christ.

These are just some glimpses of the way that open-air preaching may be used as a means of evangelism. In that context information could be imparted, and a Christian attitude to the national or local news could be evoked. Yet the real purpose was to persuade people who were not Christians to become Christians. I cannot claim that this activity resulted in many conversions, although there were a few, but it did put the various Central Halls on the map, and gave a Christian voice in opposition to the growing secularisation of our national culture.

Yours, as ever,
Dad

From: Andy Frost
To: Rob Frost
CC: Ronald Frost; Chris Frost
Subject: A Vision for Mission

Dear Dad,

What a state this nation is in! I can't understand how the church of previous generations has so failed to spread the good news. Now we are left with only a dwindling number of Christians in my generation with this mammoth job. Even now resources are not given to new mission objectives but are frittered away on dilapidated buildings and dying congregations.

This country is in desperate need of God. The statistics on youth suicide are shocking. People are searching for meaning and they cannot find it in materialism. People are searching for acceptance and they cannot find it in our cynical culture, plagued with family breakdown. People are searching for stability and cannot find it in the transience of postmodernity. People are searching for spirituality but cannot find it in crystals and horoscopes. What a key time for the church to rise triumphant, showing love that cannot be bought and grace beyond all understanding.

But the missionary heart of the church is lost and one of the biggest causes of this is that for years we have been watering down truth. In a desperate bid to appease all with a politically correct theology, the church has watered down the message of the cross. It claims that all religions lead to the same God and embraces a theory that moral conduct should be measured against the mean in society rather than a desire for complete holiness.

Jesus did not claim to be 'a' way to the Father but 'the' way, 'the' truth and 'the' life. The gospel is offensive and it is controversial but we have been given this message to take into the world and we cannot change the core fundamental truths of it. The power and urgency of the gospel are lost if we do not fully believe that Jesus died and rose again to show his love and offer us a relationship with the Father. Once we fully understand the gospel and its importance; once we let God transform us into new creations and once we accept the Holy Spirit into our lives, we should become contagious Christians once again!

People from older generations talk on about the greatness of Wesley, Spurgeon and Booth – yet all these men were radical revolutionaries in their time with a deep-seated passion to see his kingdom come. They have been remembered as great preachers but not as great evangelists. The word evangelist has almost become dirty, as we associate the term with a man standing on a street-corner shouting 'The end is nigh!' or a smartly dressed American caught in another scandal.

Jesus was a revolutionary. He hated religiosity, describing the Pharisees as whitewashed tombs with nothing but death inside. Yet somehow the church manages to portray Jesus (who made a whip and turned over tables in the temple) as boring and tame. Christianity has become religious tradition without any bite.

We need to preach the true Jesus – all man and all God. We need to preach the Jesus who cared for the prostitutes and the poor, the Jesus who raised the dead and healed the sick, the Jesus who paid the ultimate price in the name of love. And as we take this message out into the world we need to deconstruct people's preconceptions and understandings of Jesus. We need to show the world that we as his disciples are not boring, irrelevant and caught up with tradition but people of love who stand for justice and live lives of integrity. In and through this we should become proud of our calling as evangelists.

The common question is 'How do we get the opportunity to preach the gospel and to share this message?' I think that the drama that you have used, Dad, has been great in sharing the message of Christ. It is amazing to think this was once seen as radical by the church! But nowadays, people don't want to come and see Christians do drama – they have been tainted by the belief that Christians can never do anything of quality. They look at church notice boards with their cheesy one-liners that are not funny to outsiders and the luminous pink paper from the 80s. How can we be seen as having anything worth saying?

We need to earn the right to share by the way that we live our lives. People came to Jesus as they saw that he was different. I want the same to be true in my life. As Moses' face shone after he had met with God, that is what I want. I want to live a life that is so full of God that people come to me and ask why. And when it comes to radical ideas, we need to really think outside of the box. Primarily we need to love unconditionally – looking at people through God's eyes rather than our own. The whole servant evangelism model that has taken off over the past few years has been so effective in showing this on a large scale – people caring for a community enough to spend time cleaning up graffiti and collecting litter.

People would say that some of the things I do are perhaps too radical. Taking out the pews in an old church building and installing skate ramps and DJs might be seen as a little too much. Yet as people came in they were asking us – 'What are you doing? This is meant to be a place of worship.' We were then able to explain that worship is not just singing songs but lifestyle – it was a real opener to some deep conversations!

As I share my faith, I always try to make an appeal for people to give their lives to Christ – even if it is just a one-on-one conversation. The church needs to change this planting seeds mentality that it has become strangled with. So many churches that plan missions expect nothing and therefore reap nothing. There is no expectancy and the idea of God as Creator and all-powerful is lost. The seed sowing mentality is so deeply embedded within our church that everybody is sowing seeds but no one ever seems to be reaping!

Much of the mundane nature of mission has come from a lack of prayer and a lack of listening. I love the story of Ananias in Acts as he is told by God to go to Saul. He was a man listening to the Father. Yet so often we fail to spend time listening; some even disbelieve that God can actually speak to us. When we realise that God wants to speak to us and when we start spending time hearing his voice we can be so much more effective. We then know who to go to, who to share with and who to pray with. This involves stepping out of comfort zones and relying upon God, just as Ananias did as he went to meet Saul the persecutor.

Stepping out of comfort zones and risk are other words that the church has to start using. Even as I lead missions today, I see the need to delegate to the younger people around me. This is so scary as I know what can go wrong and the problems that can be caused. But I know that I cannot hold onto the power as previous generations have done; empowering others is key if the church is to move on.

Dad, your evangelistic heart is great – I think it is great what you have done in terms of mission as you have pioneered new models of evangelism. And it is amazing to think that I am another generation following in your footsteps. I long for the church to realise its calling and to take it seriously!

All in all the church remains generally apathetic. Too many committees and meetings stop us from being visionary. When it comes to mission, an Alpha course seems to suffice and meanwhile the size of the mission field is ever growing. There is only one hope for the future of mission in Britain and it comes down to another great move of God. We need to start tugging on his robes desiring that we should get a glimpse of what has happened before – a fresh anointing. Let's get passionate for more of him.

Ever desiring more,
Andy

From: Chris Frost
To: Rob Frost
CC: Ronald Frost; Andy Frost;
Subject: A Vision for Mission

Dear Dad,

I guess I've always been an evangelist; I can remember the night I recommitted my life to Jesus I got entwined in a lengthy debate with two guys in their twenties about how God was a God of love despite the suffering they had been through. I was totally out of my depth but totally in love with Jesus and couldn't contain what I'd found. I think that throughout my Christian life this was the most natural piece of mission I've ever been involved in. I had no sure-fire method or strong theological grounding but I had a passion to make the name of Jesus famous. I appreciate I've got a long way to go in understanding mission but I know that I've been fed a lot of lies and experienced a lot of truth on my journey so far.

I think the biggest lie I've ever been thrown about mission is that 'You can save people.' As a spiritual baby I was convinced that if I just pushed hard enough anyone could crack. I would feel so guilty if I hadn't at least shared my testimony with someone throughout the week, it often seemed as if I was in a conversion competition. I can remember trying to force my supposed freedom on to people whenever I could but the annoying thing was that nothing ever seemed to happen. I definitely think my most important lesson so far has been that only God can save. But I don't just sit back and let God do it because I know great things can happen when we go on partnership with Jesus in mission.

One of the closest missions to my heart was one to a small village near Barnsley. I was in charge of a group of

about fifteen guys and we were coming to the end of
the week we were there. We had been running a youth
drop-in for some local kids: just offering games of pool
and a friendly atmosphere. We had made some spiritual
leeway but that night as we gathered to pray for the
kids, before they arrived, God put a deep cry in our
hearts to call out for his mercy, a bit like the cry of Moses.
That night we lay prostrate on the dusty chapel floor
and pleaded for God to come . . . and he did! That night
God's presence filled the minister's vestry at the back of
the church and the kids were literally drawn into it. God
was moving in such a powerful way and many lives
were transformed. I learnt that night that successful mission starts in humble prayer and that it's all for the glory
of God (there's so much truth in those cheesy sayings!).
It was such a privilege to be involved in that night and I
will treasure that memory for ever.

The numbers that met Jesus that night were great and
my heart always wants more and more but I know that
we're called to make disciples. There are so many sobering
stories of new converts withering away when the spiritual emotion fades and it's something we evangelists have
got to remember when we paint a city red with the gospel.
I think anyone with a decent set of communication skills
can persuade a few people to come to the front of a church
and accept Jesus as their Saviour but if these guys are
traced in a few years time, would they be rocking it for
Jesus? We've got to learn to be patient with the harvest and
reap the crop at the right time. And it's frustrating, I know,
because we want people to share in the feast we're going
to have but commitment needs to mean commitment.

One of my favourite passages in the Bible is when
Elijah challenges all these worshippers of foreign gods to
pray for some wood to be set on fire supernaturally. He
starts taking the Mickey when nothing happens, saying

stuff like 'Shout louder, maybe they can't hear you!' Then
Elijah calls to the God of Israel to send the fire on his pile
of wood (which he's just covered with jug fulls of water)
and the thing erupts into flames. I really believe that we
don't rely enough on the power of God in mission . . .
after all doesn't it say in Acts: 'The Holy Spirit produced
signs and wonders to prove that the message was true.' It
seems today that the Wow! style of evangelism is reserved
for those amazingly spiritual, revival-dreaming celebrity
Christians that you read about in books . . . but the Word
clearly paints a picture of Jesus' disciples releasing
demons and healing the sick, when some of them weren't
even fully sure if Jesus was the Son of God! I've become
more and more convicted about the role of the Holy Spirit
in evangelism. I guess one of the birthing times for this
was just a few months after getting saved.

I was sitting on a bus waiting to get home after a great
night out with some mates. The bus was full of rowdy students all nattering away. Without warning my Christian
mate sitting next to me suddenly burst out in worship to
God. I was highly embarrassed but suddenly God's presence seemed to jump onto me and no matter how hard I
tried, I couldn't stop myself from worshipping God at the
top of my voice. His beauty had to receive recognition. The
next thing I knew I was on my feet on top of this red dou-
ble-decker and was sharing my story on how God had
transformed my life and that this was available to anyone
who would believe in Jesus. Things started happening;
questions and conversations erupted around the bus, it was
an awesome spectacle and I wish that I could claim some
recognition for it but it was all the work of God's Holy
Spirit. From that day on I knew I could trust in the Holy
Spirit's help in mission . . . and he and I have been working
together ever since, whether it's approaching those who are
ready to hear or having the faith to pray for healing.

I think the latest lesson I've learnt about evangelism is love. When I think of Jesus' life of mission I get this image of such perfect love. You could imagine him just catching your eye and imparting a thousand words without even opening his mouth. So many evangelists seem so rude and inconsiderate and there's definitely some room for that confrontational style but I've come to realise that when I'm with my mates this trait isolates rather than embraces them. So often I'd catch myself only loving those who showed an interest in my faith . . . whereas Jesus taught grace, and a love that knows no conditions!

I guess I don't want to label mission as a thing I go on any more but a life I live: a life that is real, that is full of grace and sensitive to the spirit, one that shouts when it's right and whispers when it needs to, one that knows it doesn't have everything sorted but has a great secret to tell.

God bless
Chris

'Mission is a life I live.'

From: Rob Frost
To: Ronald Frost
CC: Andy Frost; Chris Frost;
Subject: A Vision for Mission

Dear Dad, Andy and Chris,

Thanks for sharing your ideas. It's clear that we're all innovative evangelists, with lots of vision and with a heart to experiment and try new things. Yet there is, at the heart of each of us, the same driving force. The old-time revivalists used to call it a burden, a concern for the lost, a heart compassion for those who have not yet found Jesus. I hope that God will increase this sense of burden among his people. For ultimately, I believe that this is a something spiritual which comes from God. I don't believe that the church can grow again unless lots

'It's clear we're all innovative evangelists.'

of us get on our knees and ask God to give us a soul burden like this.

I do see signs of this kind of burden in the lives of many younger Christians today. When I see them, like your team crying out to God on the dusty chapel floor, Chris, I know that the church in the UK has a future. Sadly, among my generation, such a passion for those who don't know Jesus seems to be sorely lacking. Perhaps the weariness of the years and the pressures of Christian service have robbed some of us of a real passion to tell others about Jesus. Perhaps we've lost a true vision for mission, preferring to play at church instead.

Rob

6

Views of the Church

From: Rob Frost
To: Ronald Frost
CC: Andy Frost; Chris Frost
Subject: Views of the Church

Dear Dad, Andy, and Chris,

I thank God for your vision, Dad, and for the way that you always saw far beyond the structures of the institutional church. Your work in the great Central Halls of Methodism was often at the cutting edge of evangelistic outreach, and you were always thinking outside the box.

People tell me that one of my spiritual gifts is that of vision, and over the years I have tried to bring that vision to be tested and, if appropriate, developed by God's people for use by the church. I'm convinced that the church moves forward through vision, and that this is a gift which the established church struggles to incorporate.

I want to encourage you, Andy and Chris, to pray for vision, to see vision and to believe in the vision that God gives you. There's no greater fulfilment than in seeing vision become reality! But I guess you need to be prepared to carry the pain of being a visionary. I have often found the church dismissive of vision, and some of my greatest struggles have been about having vision rejected and marginalized.

That happened when I put forward the vision of the first Easter People. It was turned down by no fewer that five national church committees and boards. Had it not been for my farmer friend Richard in Yorkshire, Easter People would never have seen the light of day.

Over Christmas 1996, following this five-fold rejection he asked me one simple question. 'Do you believe this vision is from God?' I nodded. 'Well, then, you must go back and ask the five committees again!' He made me kneel down while he prayed that God would give me fresh confidence, and that the Lord would protect the vision that he had given. I returned to London with a new determination to see that vision become reality, and over the next few weeks all of the Boards and Committees changed their vote and the first Easter People was launched the following year.

The church of which you are part, Andy and Chris, must find the space to release young leaders to try new things, and give them loads of encouragement to innovate. It must help visionary mission entrepreneurs to have a go, and encourage them – even when they fail! The hallmark of the rising church must be a willingness to take risks.

The great missionary exploits of church history have never been managed by consensus. They have usually come from lone pioneers who have seen a vision and have preferred to die rather than deny it. Visionaries hold the key to the church's future, but by nature they are impatient people. They will not hang around while large organisations wait endlessly for consensus. If the church prevaricates the moment will pass and the opportunity will be missed.

The church of your generation, Andy and Chris, must learn how to release visionaries to come up with new ideas and then get behind them in implementing those ideas. The church in the UK desperately needs leaders who can receive new vision from God and who can involve others in the creation of a strategy to fulfil it. Leaders who can make a mental leap which takes what is now into what could be.

So, may I encourage you both to pray for vision? Maybe you could start by praying the prayer of Jabez – 'Too many of us have set our borders too close to our own back yard.' We live in our own pre-selected comfort zone, and shiver at the thought of God wanting to do anything more through us tomorrow than he did before. My hope is that you will constantly have a burden to extend the territory of God's Kingdom. Ultimately, however, vision is not enough. Vision without action is merely a dream. It's vision with action which can change the world. God bless you, and may he give you big vision . . . and the perseverance to see it through!

Rob.

From: Ronald Frost
To: Rob Frost
CC: Andy Frost; Chris Frost
Subject: View of the Church

Dear Robert,

I have been hearing about Café church, and the way that it has been attracting people to worship God on a Sunday evening who otherwise might feel that more traditional services did not meet their spiritual needs. I really ought to make the effort to come over one Sunday evening and experience the blessing for myself, but as far as I can make out, some forty or more young men and women gather round café style tables and have a meal together.

While sitting at the tables, the groups thus formed are encouraged to discuss some aspect of the Christian faith. Whilst waiting for the courses of the meal to be served, cabaret items are performed. These could take the form of a Bible reading, a song or other musical item, a piece of drama, a Christian testimony or a dance routine. At the end of the meal, the substance of what one might call the sermon is presented as an after dinner speech, which leads on to conversation and questioning, and ultimately to prayer.

I believe I am right in saying that this way of concluding Sundays has been envisaged by Jacqui and yourself, and has been taken up enthusiastically by both Andrew and Christopher. Apparently in their later teenage years, when ordinary church services and youth group events had begun to lose their appeal, they felt free to bring their friends to a weekly event such as this. Obviously I can see the value of all of this, and no doubt the Holy Spirit has given the initial inspiration and guided its development. I am grateful that it is happening, and that it has been used to retain the interest of young adults in the Christian faith, at a time when church attendances throughout the United Kingdom are, generally speaking, falling.

One of the things that particularly delights me is that the use of the word church, has apparently not prevented recruitment. So many modern evangelical movements would have disguised their motives by avoiding such a traditional word as 'church', but because it is a biblical word, I am glad that in this instance it has been retained. In the Greek language, in which the New Testament of the Bible was written, of course, the word used for church is *ekklesia*. This meant 'those who are called together'. The term described any formal meeting within the Roman Empire. If the town council had to meet, or the Senate itself, heralds would be sent out to call together those who were eligible to attend.

When Jesus said, 'And upon this rock I will build my church,' he was indicating that he did not only want his followers to go out into the world to be evangelists; he also wanted them to come together. It is that gathering together which is the church and, not unnaturally, gradually the place where the gatherings were held was given the same name. I have been grateful for that over the years. Any church, whatever its denominational label, I think, should be the place where it could be rightly expected that the people who Jesus had called together could be found.

Anyone encountering those people would probably find them engaged in several specific activities, and it is those activities that I have come to regard as the function of the church throughout my life.

The first of these is the worship of God. I have to confess that this has not always appeared to me as a priority. There were times when I liked to join a large congregation because I enjoyed 'a good sing'. There have been times when I have decided to attend Church A rather than Church B, because I wanted to hear a 'good sermon'.

I know I shall be called old-fashioned but I do not like the modern tendency of applauding items in an act of worship. Increasingly, I find that if someone sings a solo, the congregation claps at the end, as they would do in a concert. In worship, however, we are not met to say to an artist, 'That was jolly good.' Rather, we are met to say to Almighty God, 'You are fantastic!' That is worship. It annoys me when I go to preach in a new place and the steward insists on introducing me to the congregation before we begin. People have not come to hear about me. Similarly I do not like going to a church where someone gives out the notices before the first hymn, on the pretext that 'We will get them out of the way, before you start.'

I'm not too happy either, with calls to worship: they don't very often seem very appropriate to me. When I was at university, I would quite often go to Westminster Central Hall. Dr. Sangster would come onto the platform, look all round that vast auditorium, and simply say, 'We are gathered to worship Almighty God, let us stand to sing . . .' One felt immediately that what we had made the journey to London to do was now under way.

My God how wonderful Thou art,
Thy Majesty how bright...

Eternal Light, Eternal Light,
How pure the soul must be,
When placed within Thy searching sight,
It shrinks not, but with calm delight,
Can live and look on Thee.

You will notice that I prefer the use of the second person singular pronoun. God is different, he is not just one of us. I really do lament the passing of the age when God was held in such reverence that we even used a different pronoun to refer to Him.

The second function of the church should be to teach people about God. There is a great opportunity to do this in the context of a Sunday service, but week-day meetings for Bible instruction are also important. Part of the success of John Wesley was his insistence on the class meeting, which he expected every Methodist to attend once a week in order to engage in Christian fellowship, prayer and Bible study.

A third function of the church should be to provide Christlike service to the community. I have been very fortunate to spend most of my ministry in the Central Missions of Methodism, where we had sufficient staff and resources to be able to assist people in need, at almost any time. That is not so fantastic as it sounds because most people who declare that they are in great need initially only want a friendly ear to whom they can pour out their troubles. Practical assistance and long term care may follow, important contacts may need to be made, but the first step is usually much more simple than that. In these hectic days, worried people are glad to find someone who will listen to them, without having to take a numbered ticket and wait for it to be called, in perhaps two hours' time.

A fourth function of the church is to evangelise. There are an enormous number of ways of doing that today, so it is strange that it seems to have such a low priority in so many churches. John Wesley's genius was in the line of his brother's hymn, 'O let me commend my Saviour to you.' It doesn't make much difference whether that is done by open-air preaching, or chatting to a group of teenagers, whose confidence has been gained in a football match: opportunities must be sought to let everyone know that being a Christian is not the same as being a law-abiding citizen.

The fifth function of the church is to provide facilities where Christian people can socialise. When we become Christians we do not give up all the normal physical and emotional needs and tendencies of human beings. There is a growing tendency today for Christians to join secular organisations in which to pursue their leisure activities. One cannot disagree with that, because a group of scuba-divers can only be improved if one of them is a Christian, and a Christian cyclist is bound to be an acquisition to a road-racing club. I have found, however, that there is also need for the church sometimes to make provision for its members to do secular things together, and that for them to meet across age groups for outings or social gatherings where there can be laughter and the sharing of various skills can enrich Christian fellowship.

I sometimes lament the passing of the church as I have known it. It was the focal point of the life of its members. Whole families belonged to a church, and because each family knew the shared values of the others, romances developed and young people pledged their troth to each other, and new Christian families were formed. The modern church is not so closely family orientated, and society itself is more fragmented, so the present generation is having to find new ways of sustaining a social element within the Christian fellowship, and it may be that Café church is one way in which this is being achieved. I therefore pray that God will bless it in every way.

One final thing, however, must be said. It does not matter how well the worship is organised, however excellent the instruction sessions are, how much time is given to social care, or how much expertise is exerted on social functions: if all of this is just well planned secular activity, it will not be successful, and it certainly won't be a church. For any group of people to be a church requires the presence of Jesus. He said, 'Where two or three are gathered together in my Name, there am I in the midst of them.' If Jesus is not in the centre of all we do, and the awareness of his presence is never felt, we may have a wonderfully organised society, but we will not have a church. 'Except the Lord build the house,' says Psalm 127, 'they labour in vain, who build it.'

Yours, as ever,
Dad

From: Andy Frost
To: Rob Frost
CC: Ronald Frost; Chris Frost
Subject: View of the Church

Dear Dad,

This year I sat in a church meeting as we talked about mission. As I sat talking to a variety of church elders, young people were congregating outside the building. I heard that the young people were desperate for something to do but that there was no money to do anything. I heard about the escalating drug problem. I heard about the young girls' pregnancies. I heard about the lack of jobs. I heard about the lack of hope. I began to weep on the inside as I sat in a meeting talking, whilst young people remained on the church doorstep with no hope and no understanding of what church was really about.

I continued talking to the church officials and then discovered that there was a rural church a few miles away with a dwindling congregation that had just learned that an old church artefact at the front of the building was worth a staggering £50,000. What had the church done? Had they sold the window and employed youth workers? Had they sold the window and built a youth centre? Had they invested the money from the windows into drug rehabilitation? No. Instead the church had forked out hundreds of pounds to insure the window yearly. My anger levels rose and I remembered Jesus in the temple and the righteous anger that he had. Was there no urgency?

For too long the church has been about buildings, meetings, traditions and Sunday mornings. The church has failed to invest in life. It should be offering life and

life to the full. It should be urgently spreading the good
news, investing in people rather than pews, loving the
community with no hidden agenda. But again and again
you see the church in maintenance mode. The church is
trying to maintain its membership rather that mission
into the surrounding area. The church is maintaining the
building rather than investing in the future. The church
is maintaining traditions rather than changing to meet
the needs of the community.

No vision means death. It is summed up in Proverbs
29:18, 'Where there is no vision, the people perish'
(Authorised Version). We need to be a people of continued vision, encouraging those with bold new ideas. So
often God has imparted vision, there is backing from
discerning friends, the finances come in and all the lights
seem green. But then suddenly the church hierarchy
steps in. They are not keen and you are thrown into
uncertainty – rather than embracing the vision of a
young person, they recoil in fear and trepidation.

The easy response is to apportion blame, point the
finger and criticise particular denominations and
churches. But that is not God's way. We are told to love
one another. Jesus' final prayer in John 17 was all about
unity – it commands a blessing! We are told to respect
our elders. So what is the answer?

I have had to repent for my wrong thoughts about the
church. In my teenage years there was no discipleship, no
freedom to dream dreams and no responsibility vested in
me, bar the Bible reading rota once a term. When I failed
to fit into the mundane style of Sunday mornings, no one
came round to visit or to talk to me. I guess everyone
thought someone else would do it. It is so easy to harbour
bitterness but I had to forgive and let go. Instead of
mulling over the shortcomings, I turned my attention to
praying. As I prayed for the church, I began to see God's

heart for my local church. The Bride should be perfect for Christ – how far we all have to go! Even in our failures we remember that he continues to love this diverse and complicated Body that is united in one Spirit.

One of the biggest problems is that we so often fail to recognise the transformations that have occurred in the past eighty years. As I struggle to use the scores of features on my mobile phone, many of the people in our churches grew up in a world without a phone in the house. As I flick through dozens of TV channels and get interactive on the web, we forget that these commodities were only dreams. With society ever moving on, it is no wonder that the older generations have desperately wanted to hold the balance of power. It is no wonder that they have wanted the comfort of old hymns rather than electric guitars. Everything has moved so fast and today knowledge is transferred up the generations rather than vice versa, the way it has been since time began!

We need to pray for traditional church and continue to love the wider family. We need caringly to encourage them to move on with God but when they fail to understand us, we need to understand the alien world that we come from – the multimedia computer age of MTV and Costa coffee. More and more, I believe that we need to support the traditional church whilst pioneering new ways of understanding this complex, multi-cultural community.

As we move into new ways of being church, we need to understand that is not about meetings but about community. I really want to get back to the simplicity of Acts – a church that 'devoted themselves to the apostles' teaching and to the fellowship, to the breaking of bread and to prayer' (Acts 2:42). How simple, yet so often we complicate the issues. The most amazing thing is that they had 'everything in common' (Acts 2:44). This is the kind of church that I would like to belong to – where everything is shared and where the aim is so clear that materialistic things fail to be important.

The key to the church in Acts is that the church was 100% involved. A recent study found that in the average church, 3% of the congregation were employed to minister, 17% were heavily involved and the other 80% had no involvement. They were just pew fillers. This is not what it should mean to be a Christian. New young leaders need to mobilise this sleeping giant. I am sure that that is why the church achieved so much in Acts. At Café church 100% involvement is key – everyone has gifts and these have to be used and continually developed.

As we move forward I can promise you that we will make mistakes – my generation is full of pioneers planting new forms of church in night clubs, surf culture and

'My generation is full of pioneers' – Andy teaches on the Dawn Patrol mission.

in the market place but there will be failures. There needs to be a recognition from the mainstream denominations that what is happening is vital and important; and that there needs to be real support for these projects. At the same time, we must recognise the rich heritage of the established church. As I continue with my Methodist local preaching course I begin to get some comprehension of the richness of formal prayers and liturgy.

My generation owes you much for what you have done – we are a testimony of what the church has achieved. At the same time, the established church needs to support and encourage an emerging generation which is pushing the boundaries that this nation might turn back to God!

Love,
Andy

From: Chris Frost
To: Rob Frost
CC: Ronald Frost; Andy Frost;
Subject: View of the Church

Dear Dad,

I've been bored, hurt, entertained, despised and trained
by the church. I've loved it, hated it, built it, abused it,
written it off and chosen to commit to it. In and out of
my walk with Jesus I've come to learn that this is what
he has chosen to express his love to a needy world. I
guess like many people of my age, I still carry a spiritual scar from local churches I've been to in the past. It
seems as if so many non-Christians I chat to, complain:
'church is dead, dull and boring; I was forced to go when
I was a kid.' My heart seems to cry; 'Yes but this isn't
what Jesus is like. If only our churches could reflect
him.'

I think one of the effects of seeing things done so
wrongly so many times is that I've been meticulously
judgemental of any new church I've attended. I feel like
an abused lover that is scared of making a new commitment. But I see that I'm lost without the company and
support of a local church, and slowly but surely, I'm having to lay past experiences at the cross and, a lot like
Andy, I've had to forgive and forget past transgressions,
and love unconditionally.

Writing a letter about the church at this time is an
especially difficult process for me. It seems that wherever I go recently, people want to introduce me to their
theological understanding of church. I feel lost in a
world of 'doing church'. The trouble is that I can see
truth in most of them. But it's not the diversity of understanding that gets on my nerves: it's the divisions that

they create. Jesus' heart was for unity; it's what he prayed for! And how will we unite? Well it's not going to be through striving for the perfect model but when we look beyond our differences and appreciate our similarities; when we celebrate our God-given gifts of diversity and when we start boasting grace rather than our most impressive convert statistics.

Jesus wants a beautiful bride. How do we become beautiful? By taking our eyes off ourselves and fixing them on the author and perfector of our faith. When the bride was used as an analogy of the church, the weddings at the time were focused around the groom and not the bride. In fact the bride would wait in anticipation for the glorious arrival of the groom. Oh, that we would take our eyes off ourselves and be transformed by the beautiful Jesus that we worship. We've spent so long in front of the mirror trying to iron out our wrinkles that we've forgotten Jesus, beautiful, beautiful Jesus. He's so wonderful, so perfect, so loving and he longs for us to get excited about him!

The Christian catchphrase at the moment seems to be 'the problem with the church is. . .' It sometimes seems as if people are trained in criticising her, they seem so good at it. But Jesus loves the church. We are the church. We need God's eyes of mercy: as church we need to look at our reflection and say; you are beautiful. And I'm not denying that we need change; we don't share everything we have, we don't love unconditionally and we don't see our numbers growing daily. But we need to be cleansed by the blood of Jesus from issues of self esteem. Let's have eyes of hope and love rather than negativity and fear.

I can remember being part of a small evangelistic team at an 'on the move' barbecue. The day was dragging a little and there weren't that many conversations

going on. Then, about half way through the day, I got
chatting to this homeless guy and then the conversation
led on to church. He told me this long drawn out story
how one church in particular had been so rude and not
cared for him. I was left feeling outraged at this supposed church! But I went on to tell him how there is
hope and how my church had catered for my needs.
Then out of the steam of one of the barbies came one of
my church leaders who he recognised . . . and then it
came clear that the church he was talking about was
mine. At first I was outraged at my church: how could it
have betrayed this poor man! But then I remembered
how much it had done for me. I guess the point I want
to make is that we've got to be careful about what we listen to about our and other churches. The devil will pull
apart anything godly in any way he can and we should
fight hard to stay united.

I've become part of a New Frontiers church in Leeds
while I've been at university and I feel as if I'm just starting to grasp their vision of doing church. I'm realising
the importance of community; I want to unlock the idea
of becoming brothers and sisters in Christ and working
with one another as a local body. And the church is
healthy, all the parts are functioning, people are released
into their visions and there is a growing sense of family.
It seems as if I'm falling in love with the reality of church
all over again! It's not perfect though and it doesn't pretend to be but every church has its strengths and weaknesses and I've got to remember that. Who knows,
maybe one day I'll start a church, but for now I know I'm
just a baby with a lot to learn.

Love,
Chris

From: Rob Frost
To: Ronald Frost
CC: Andy Frost; Chris Frost;
Subject: View of the Church

Dear Dad, Andy and Chris,

As I look out of the Devon window where I am writing I can see the tower and walls of an ancient church. It has stood there for centuries, an immovable pillar in society. Its very architecture speaks of stability and security. Every Sunday morning its bells echo across the town, calling the faithful to worship. The gospel is faithfully preached there, and every Sunday people from across the town make their way to worship.

In my mind's eye I can see a raft of new churches which are springing up all over the country. Arts churches, youth churches, surf churches, student churches, house churches, purpose driven churches and pub churches. And now we have 'liquid expressions of church' whose structure is fluid and constantly changing . . . a network of relationships focussed on Jesus. Many of these would be unrecognisable to you, Dad, but they do still encompass many of your core definitions of what church is!

Maybe we're in the middle of a revolution in church. It's a confusing picture, and it's hard to see what the future will hold. One thing's for sure, however, it's Christ's church and not ours. He is doing a new thing, and I'm thrilled that we're all a part of shaping what is yet to be. I'm excited about the future of the church.

After generations of dormant slumber it's waking up again. Out of the dead traditions and dusty rituals a new church is emerging. I hope that God will give us the personal flexibility and adaptability to embrace what's coming . . . whatever shape it takes!

God bless,
Rob

7

Regrets Across the Years

From: Rob Frost
To: Ronald Frost
CC: Andy Frost; Chris Frost
Subject: Regrets Across the Years

Dear Dad, Andy and Chris,

As you know, I ran an annual short-term summer mission programme for over fifteen years. It was called Share Jesus, and every year hundreds of young people joined me for a week of front-line mission and evangelism. It was the highlight of my year and one of the most important aspects of my ministry. During the Millennium, the mission was in London and I was looking for the biggest team ever.

So how do you think I felt when Mike Pilavachi announced that he was taking twenty thousand Soul Survivor punters on mission to Manchester for Vision 2000? And how do you think I felt when I heard that some of my key leaders had switched their effort and energy to Manchester, rather than London? And how do you think I felt when I compared Soul Survivor's expensive high gloss publicity to our own?

Gutted. Upset. Angry. Threatened. Fed up. Puzzled.
Annoyed. Exasperated. Choleric. Ill at ease. And what
did some of my most trusted friends in Share Jesus say?
They said . . . 'Tough, Rob.'

I decided to contact Mike Pilavachi to tell him how I
felt. But when I met him and heard his vision I recognised how wrong I'd been. It was a great meeting, a
sweet time of fellowship between brothers having the
same heart, sharing the same vision, and carrying the
same burden. And from that conversation came a relationship which meant that when Soul Survivor brings
thousands of missioners to London, that Share Jesus will
be part of the team . . . and that you, Andy and Chris,
will both be among the key leaders! I really do admire
Mike and the team for what they're doing. It's a vision
far bigger than my own. And I'm glad that they're
really going for it.

Looking back over the years, I have often wrestled with
what I can only describe as a competitive spirit. I've
wanted to be the best, to do my best and to achieve the most
and, while these may be admirable qualities in themselves,
they can also tempt us to compare ourselves with others,
seeking to outdo them and to beat the competition. I'm sure
that these temptations will be as real to you in the development of your ministry as they have been to me over the last
twenty years in mine. I've come to understand that one of
the hallmarks of really godly leadership is a kind of big-
heartedness which really does love the opposition!

When I was an angry young man (some years ago
now!) I gathered a group of similar impatient young
Christians around me to start a little event which you
now help to organise that's called Easter People. Out
of courtesy, I contacted Spring Harvest to share my
ideas. After all, I was planning to hold my event at
exactly the same time of year. To my surprise and

apprehension they summoned me to their next full Executive.

What happened there will remain with me for ever. I guess I'd expected acrimony, anger, or some persuasive offer of partnership. Not a bit of it. The whole executive asked me to kneel, and as I knelt before them, they laid hands on me and prayed God's richest blessing on me and on the new radical event of which I'd dreamed. I was moved to tears. That, to me, was a great example of Christian leadership. I saw that my heroes like Peter Meadows, Clive Calver and Dave Pope were big enough and bold enough to say to a little upstart like me, 'Go for it . . . and go with our blessing.' In so doing, they modelled all the very best in the leadership of the church.

I'm sure that in both your ministries, Andy and Chris, some of your best ideas will be used by others: some of your best people will be poached by other organisations: sometimes when you're planning a mission in an area you will be 'gazumped' by people you thought were allies: and even if you don't have a competitive spirit your ministry will be undermined by others who do! There will be many times when you'll have to exercise grace rather than your rights.

Over the years I have watched you in your ministry, Dad. You have been hurt many times, but you have always kept on keeping on. I hope that I can continue with the same determination. And I hope that both of you, Andy and Chris, will press ahead with all the exciting plans for mission which you have, but don't ever think of it as a business. For we serve a different agenda and we are owned by a Servant King.

One day John came busy-bodying to Jesus and said . . . 'Teacher, we saw a man driving out demons in your name and we told him to stop, because he was not one of us.' But Jesus replied . . . 'Do not stop him. No-one who does a miracle in my name can in the next moment say anything bad about me, for whosoever is not against us is for us.' In other words . . . 'Tough.' My Jesus is always ready to affirm the good; always looking for new leaders to build his church. Always planting new visions. Always spreading his word in new ways. And his resurrection life has an unstoppable way of getting round those who try to kill off his work.

So keep your vision, go for the goals which the Lord has set you. But always encourage those who are doing the same work, fighting the same fight, seeking the same result . . . because that is part of what makes Christian ministry so different. I'm genuinely sorry for any competitive spirit which has tarnished my ministry. And, looking at the collaborative way in which you work, I don't think it will tarnish yours.

God bless,
Rob

From: Ronald Frost
To: Rob Frost
CC: Andy Frost; Chris Frost
Subject: Regrets Across the Years

Dear Robert,

I expect that you remember the farming incident that Ma often used as a children's address in a Sunday morning service. She used to say that during the Second World war, some German prisoners of war were sent to work on her father's farm in the Cotswold hills. Finding one who could speak English better than the rest, her father thought that he would train him to use the horse-plough.

Having shown him how to harness the horse and install him between the shafts, and how to adjust the depth of the cutting edge of the plough, he then said to the German, 'In order to get the furrows straight, you must keep your eye on the corner of the cow shed and steer the plough handles directly towards it.'

Visiting the field again later in the morning, Mr. Williams saw the field ploughed but with furrows that zigzagged and curved all over the place. They were anything but straight. He was a patient old gentleman and asked the inexperienced ploughman why he had not carried out his instruction and kept his eye on the immovable corner of the cow shed. With embarrassment, he got the reply, 'I'm sorry sir, I thought you said, "Keep your eye on the horn of the cow's head."'

It was never discovered whether the prisoner was trying to damage the British harvest or whether he genuinely misunderstood the instructions, but the point of the story being told in Christian worship was that if anyone keeps their eyes on Jesus, that person's life will be straight; but if anyone's life is not directed towards Jesus, the chaos of sin will result.

You have asked me to set down mistakes and regrets along the way. Individually they would be too numerous to mention, but collectively I can sum them up in Ma's story. I regret those times when I have taken my eyes off Jesus. It is those times, when I have – as the Methodist Covenant Service says – 'followed the desires and devices of my own heart' that things have gone wrong.

Self analysis has never been one of my strong points. I preferred John Wesley's instructions for the Band Meeting. This was only open to those who were thought to be more mature in the Christian faith than those who met in class. The requirement was that they should be willing to be told their faults, and 'that right good and home!'

It may be that if those with whom I have worked and to whom I have ministered were asked to write this letter, they would see my sins very differently, but from my perspective, when I have taken my eyes off Jesus I have been proud, impatient and bad tempered. If I were to catalogue every such incident much more space would be required than is available here, but perhaps I could illustrate what I mean by something that has cropped up several times during my ministry. That is my relationship with my organists.

I like the old-fashioned gospel songs, made famous in *Sacred Songs and Solos*, more popularly called *Sankey's 1200*. The tunes seem to me to be simple, they seem to fit the mood of the words, and have the kind of beat to which most people can relate. Moreover, most of them had a chorus to be sung after each verse, so that a Christian truth could be emphasised on minds that had been occupied with non-religious thoughts most of the week. Supremely, if anyone got fascinated by the thought of that chorus, it could be repeated again after the last verse!

One of the most essential things in a Methodist Central Hall is the installation of an excellent and expensive organ. This, of course, requires the appointment of an absolutely first class musician who can handle such an instrument. First class musicians, however, do not always like Mr. Moody's music, to which Ira D. Sankey's hymns were often set. This situation, alas, has more than once caused disharmony between my organists and myself. I have usually insisted that the preacher is in charge of the service, and is likely to know the needs of the congregation better than the organist. The organist, usually supported by the members of the choir, has attacked my lack of musical knowledge, and insisted that nothing but the best should be employed in the worship of God, and that the music that I have wanted to use is quite sub-standard.

The verbal exchanges that can take place when people argue from such differently held positions can become quite unworthy of those who are supposed to be brothers and sisters in Christ, and whenever such a situation has arisen, I have been left wondering . . .'how I can be worthy to lead others in worship, when I am so lacking in holiness myself?'

Sometimes this has led me to apologise, but more often I have insisted that I am in the right, and strained relationships and even resignations have resulted. Looking back, I can do nothing but regret such occurrences. In later life, I hope I have found the advice of St Paul in Ephesians chapter 4, verse 26, more applicable; 'Let not the sun go down on your wrath.' I do, however, have to be penitent for those times when my own self-importance has been a bad example of the spreading of the love of Christ.

I am sure that you will understand that the example that I have given does not mean to indicate that all my disputes have been with church organists. Stewards, secretaries, youth leaders, temperance workers, tradespeople, shop assistants, students, colleagues, family members and goodness knows how many more people have similarly suffered, because I took my eyes off Jesus, and – going my own way instead – became proud and bad-tempered.

The words of John Henry Newman, in his well known hymn are so appropriate in my own case:

> Lead kindly Light amid the encircling gloom
> Lead Thou me on,
> I was not ever thus nor prayed that Thou
> Should'st lead me on.
> I loved to choose and see my path; but now
> Lead Thou me on.
> I loved the garish day, and spite of fears,
> Pride ruled my will. Remember not past years.

It is the last four words of that verse which are the most important; the plea that God will not remember my self will, my personal choice and my pride. Of course he will not. He has promised, in Jeremiah chapter 31 and verse 34, 'I will forgive their iniquity and remember their sin no more.' I hope that I have ultimately made my peace with those people with whom I have had fierce disagreements over the years.

In the last resort, however, our sins do not just affect human relationships. We must never forget that God is holy, and that if the way we live is an affront to God's holiness, we need his forgiveness as well. Fortunately, that grace, if we are truly penitent, is guaranteed. Jesus prayed, 'Father forgive them,' as he hung upon the cross. At least that's where my ultimate peace lies, and I should like to commend it to anyone else who reviews their life, and finds it besmirched by sin of any kind.

If I take my eyes off Jesus, my life goes all crooked, and I sin. I must then try to make amends with those who have been hurt, but I must never forget that I hurt God as well. His pardon is available for anyone who is truly penitent. It is already guaranteed because,

> There is a green hill far away
> Outside a city wall
> Where the dear Lord was crucified,
> Who died to save us all.
>
> He died that we might be forgiven . . .

He died that I might be forgiven. That's where my heart rests, and I believe yours does, too. I desperately want to commend that forgiveness, and the rest it brings, to others.

Much love,
Dad

From: Andy Frost
To: Rob Frost
CC: Ronald Frost; Chris Frost
Subject: Regrets Across the Years

Dear Dad,

I am not sure if I ever told you about my sailing adventure. One of my mates from university is a keen sailor and has forever been trying to get me to go sailing with him. Eventually, after years of nagging, I finally agreed to join him. With the picture in my head of a great white yacht – the kind that you would find in St Tropez – with a sunny day, a gentle breeze and the sipping of champagne as my buddy steered the ship in turquoise water, I began to get quite excited.

The actual trip was slightly different to my imagined fairy tale. The sailing boat was more of a dinghy and the Thames estuary was not quite the Caribbean. Nevertheless, we set off kitted up with life vests and waterproofs to sail into a force 7. The next thing I know, we are bouncing from side to side of this boat, which is almost at right angles as we are jibbing up the river, knocking around in a couple of feet of chop. Within moments I am beginning to feel sick and my romanticised idea of sailing is ruined forever! It was at this point that my friend tells me to focus on the horizon and all will be well. As I focused upon the horizon which never moved, it helped me to regain perspective and the sickness was soon alleviated.

Focus is so important. Christian ministry is more like being in the dinghy than the St Tropez yacht. People have the idea that being in 'Christian work' is easy, with lots of time for a spiritual life and all your energy spent on Jesus-centred projects. Yet as soon as you are in the cut and thrust of the Christian world, the picture can look very different. You start to see the pressures upon organisations to bring in the right number of people. You begin to see that if an event is not growing, then it is destined for the slag heap. Then there are the financial pressures as you struggle to make ends meet in a competitive market place.

With ever increasing deadlines and the need to get everything done well, the pressures are immense and too often I find my focus is no longer on Jesus but on the waves and the rocking boat. I begin to worry about the increasing work-load and struggle to find the time to meet with God before I preach the next sermon. It is so easy to start serving breadcrumbs rather than putting the effort into hot crusty loaves.

I love the story of Peter walking on water (Mt. 14: 22–33). Jesus comes to the disciples in the boat,

'The cut and thrust of the Christian world can be so different.' Andy preaches in a school in Ghana.

walking along the lake. At first the disciples are afraid but Jesus says 'Take courage.' What a comforting thought! We need to have our eyes focused upon Jesus because he is our power source. Throughout history, he has been doing the impossible, saving Daniel from lions, parting seas, burning soaking wet altars, equipping ordinary fishermen to preach, making whales spew up men, raising the dead . . . Our focus has to be on Jesus – the Alpha and Omega, the Beginning and the End. He is so much more than a warm fuzzy feeling when we worship. He is so much more than 'My Jesus, my Saviour'. He is God and our focus needs to be on him, as he is the power that we need to rely on if we want him to do great things through us.

Peter then challenges Jesus to call him out of the boat. What an obscure request, but I guess that Peter just wanted to be with Jesus. The most amazing thing is that Jesus then says to him 'Come'. The next thing we know, Peter is stepping down from the boat and is starting to do the impossible. He is beginning to walk on water!

We need to focus upon Jesus because he has the plan. I love Jesus' prayer to the Father in John 17, when he prays that 'as I have been sent into the world, so have I sent them.' The great Commission reinforces the fact that he has chosen to send us into the world to change history. As Peter steps out of the boat, so must we step out of comfort zones, out of our church services and our safe Christian environment. Jesus is calling us into the world to be salt and light but we must be focused upon Jesus because he has the plan. As the sheep hear the shepherd, so we must follow his call.

As Peter is walking, he suddenly begins to take notice of the waves and the wind. When he does so, he begins to sink. As his focus is taken from Jesus and onto the problems, he stops doing the impossible and needs rescuing. Yet Jesus does not leave him floundering but grabs Peter and saves him. We need to focus upon Jesus because he has paid the price. Our God is slow to anger and quick to forgive.

My greatest sorrow is for the times when I have taken my focus from Jesus and concentrated on the things of this world. Too often I am limited in what I do because I spend more time 'doing' rather than 'being'. My focus is upon my short comings, my failures, my lack of holiness. rather than who I am in Christ – a child of God. My focus is not on the awesome Jesus who has the power to do the spectacular and the amazing despite my inadequacies.

At other times, I am sorry for the ways in which I haven't wanted to change to fulfil the great plan. Times when I have not wanted to leave the boat and have in fact gripped ever tighter to the seat. Sometimes through fear and sometimes through apathy: always because my focus has not been on him but upon myself.

At times, my focus can switch to the things of this world. The waves that I want to surf and the things that I want to do grab my attention. Sometimes I have been foolish with decisions that I have made with girls and my focus has not been on him. When you read passages such as Philippians 2 v 5-8, 'Your attitude should be that of Christ Jesus; who, being in very nature God, did not consider equality with God something to be grasped, but made himself nothing, taking the very nature of a servant, being made in human likeness. And being found in appearance as a man, he humbled himself and became obedient to death – even death on a cross', you realise just how far you still have to go. There is so much of this world that we still hold on to and so much that we must let go of in order to get our focus on Jesus again. The greatest thing is that no matter how far we have fallen and how far we have strayed from his path, his arms are always open and he is waiting to save us from the murky waters of destruction.

The English language is really lacking in words for 'sorry'. We use the same word to apologise when we accidentally bump into someone as we do when we give our condolences to someone who has lost a loved one. We say 'sorry' for being late and 'sorry' to end a relationship. The word is so commonly used, often without any meaning or depth of understanding. He wants so much more than a word, he wants our lives.

As I battle to keep the focus on Jesus in my own relationship and in my ministry, I feel that this is the biggest problem we all face. It seems that some previous generations of Christians have had their focus on social action, moral teaching, church history and fund raising. All of these are great, but if Jesus is not the focus, then they will never achieve anything long-term for Christ. The church needs to put the focus back on Jesus! And this begins with a time of repentance.

But perhaps my generation is also in danger of getting the focus wrong. We have seen so many great developments in youth worship and teaching but my fear is that sometimes we begin to worship 'worship' and 'big speakers'. I pray that these do not become idols but that they will continue to be the means of getting our focus fully and completely on Jesus.

As Colossians 3:2 says, 'Set your minds on things above, not on earthly things.' Lord God, this is my prayer.

Andy

From: Chris Frost
To: Rob Frost
CC: Ronald Frost; Andy Frost
Subject: Regrets Across the Years

Dear Dad,

I can remember when I was nine and found in my hands the very latest in modern warfare armoured vehicles, the best any child could ask for; a G.I. Joe armoured tank complete with firing missiles, straight from America and a gift for me! My young eyes widened in disbelief and a shiver of excitement ran down my spine. Without any warning I was off, ripping the box apart to uncover my new gift.

I'm pretty ashamed when I look back at that moment and realise just how rude and inconsiderate I was: there was no hug, no thank you, no smile: nothing to show my appreciation. 'But you would understand! You wouldn't mind.' But it was the least you deserved, you had done your very best for me, taken every care to see to my needs. And as I reminisce about my rudeness I'm reminded of our generation. Your generation has done so much for us; done the best to teach us what you know and pass down the baton of responsibility at the right time. How often have we run off with what you have given us with no sign of appreciation, no heartfelt gratitude or thank you?

When I ran off and unscrambled the packaging, I realised things weren't going to be as easy as I had thought: The tank needed assembling and, after two or three pride-filled hours, the fully equipped and ready to fire fighting machine was a pile of broken plastic – what had I done! How long has our generation run off with the harvest you have prepared, expecting we can do it on our own? We have been like the prodigal son, so keen to do things our way that we have forgotten the Father and the wisdom he holds. I just pray that we don't end up amongst the pig fodder before we realise what we've done. The time has come for us to swallow our pride, come to you with our broken pieces and say 'Father, we have sinned against heaven and before you. Won't you forgive us and embrace us again?'

I can remember taking part in an all-age mission a year or so ago and, during the final meeting, I had been asked to share some of my experiences from the week. Before taking the microphone I was running through a miracle list of that week. I'd seen God move in some marvellous ways and here it was, the chance I'd been waiting for – some time to tell those 'old fogies' what God can do! Several hundred old people sat in silence as

'I shakily picked up the mike.'

I approached the microphone. In my head I was psyching myself up as if I was about to enter a boxing ring, and then suddenly God spoke these words to me: 'It's only through the prayers and love of that generation that you are here today.' The words melted my heart instantly as God's warmth came over me. I shakily picked up the mike, now almost in tears and wondered what to say. I looked to Jesus for inspiration and this is what I murmured: 'I've seen God move in some incredible ways this week and it's really blown my socks off, but for me it just keeps coming back to God's grace and that he would not only love, but use sinners like us. But today I really want to honour and thank the older generation represented here today for being obedient to God in your lives and for bringing us up in all your love and prayers.'

That was a humbling experience. There's been so many times like that when I suddenly realise that I don't have it all sorted and that I've got so much to learn from guys who've been battling in the faith for much longer than me. I might have the passion and the energy but without the wisdom I'm just going to deflate like a helium balloon. Every week or so I meet with a kind of spiritual father figure called Mike from my local church and for a lot of the time I just seem to stare at him in wonder. Being subjected to such a strong faith which has passed so many trials and tribulations is humbling and as I sit and eat with him, my heart seems to say . . . together! As generations together we can get there; we can encourage and sharpen one another, help each other when times are tough and share things we have learnt. And I know that it's got to be an emergence of real friendships across the generations to mould us together rather than just religious meetings. But I do long for it and I'm just so sorry for when I've hindered it.

Dad, I want to take this opportunity to thank you for what you have done and to say sorry for getting so involved with the glamour of God's work rather than the humility and unity of it. When will I realise that God uses the good, not the great? Oh Jesus, would you humble our generation and bring us back to our roots. The time has come.

Chris

From: Rob Frost
To: Ronald Frost
CC: Andy Frost; Chris Frost
Subject: Regrets Across the Years

Dear Dad, Andy and Chris,

We are all flawed, and it's clear that there is much that we regret. If we were to go in for personal introspection big time, this book would not be big enough to cover a week of our regrets . . . let alone a lifetime! There is much, I'm sure, of which we're ashamed, and it's best that many things are left between ourselves and the good Lord. Yet what we've shared gives a tiny indication of the kind of failings that we have, and the kind of mistakes we've made.

Last year I stood on a beach in Galilee with you, Dad, and with you, Chris. We remembered that this was probably the place where the risen Jesus cooked fish for Peter. This little pebble beach beside the still waters of Galilee may well have been where Jesus asked Peter 'Do you love me?' This was, for Peter, the one who had denied his friend and master, the beach of reconciliation, the beach of new beginnings.

It's just as well that the gospel of Jesus is a gospel of new beginnings: and that the good news of forgiveness which we share with others is good news for us, too. We are fallen people, and we have all made many mistakes. On the Last Day every secret will be made known, and we'll only be able to stand before him because of his Calvary love . . . and not because of anything we've done.

I really struggle to understand what John Wesley meant when he spoke of 'entire sanctification' or 'perfect love'. I guess it's about a hunger to be more like Jesus and asking the Lord to change us and to transform us into his image. It's about feeling that we've failed, we're unworthy, and we're broken. It's about standing on the beach with Peter, and hearing him say 'Do you love me more than this other stuff?' And, just like Peter, it's about standing in a place of new beginnings. It's discovering that we are still loved, still accepted.

And then we hear the words . . . 'Feed my sheep. Feed my lambs.' It's time to go and serve him again.

God bless,
Rob

8

Walking with the Lord

From: Rob Frost
To: Ronald Frost
CC: Andy Frost; Chris Frost
Subject: Walking with the Lord

Dear Dad, Andy and Chris,

Time and again over the years, by phone or letter, you've all assured me of your prayers, and I know that this was no idle promise. You've stood behind me in prayer like a faithful family should.

I've often lived with a sense of failure that my prayer life has been 'below par'. I readily admit that, after more that twenty-five years of Christian ministry I'm convinced that there is much more to the spiritual life than I've yet discovered, and I'm hungry for more! Over the last couple of years I've been making a journey towards the deep and mysterious places that the Lord has prepared for me. I think I've lived for years under a great cloud of guilt about my Christian spirituality. Looking back I feel that some Christian leaders have put great weights on me about the devotional life, weights which Jesus never intended me to carry.

My reading of Jesus' teaching on prayer in the Sermon on the Mount is that, first and foremost, he wants my prayer life to be real, not make-believe. It's not something for show nor is it my means of salvation. And my prayers are certainly not made more acceptable because of their length! I've come to believe more and more that what God's looking for is integrity and sincerity. He is looking for my heart's desire to get to know him and to communicate with him. He's looking for my willingness to share my innermost secrets with him. Ultimately he wants to know that I really do want to stand in his presence.

I don't believe that the heart of Christian devotion is discipline, as I was always taught. It's integrity. It's not 'I'd better have a quiet time for ten minutes' but 'I really do want to meet the living God!' He's looking for heart, not duty.

For me, prayer begins with relaxing in the presence of God. A decent armchair, a mug of hot tea, and the creation of a fenced off period of time in which I won't be disturbed is crucial. Then I turn to rest and be still in his presence, and to worship the Lord for who he is, the God of all things. No-one taught me how to 'practise the presence of God', but I find that it's something which is as natural as breathing. The best advice I ever read on this subject is found in one of the greatest seventeenth century classics on prayer called *Experiencing the depths of Jesus Christ*.[1] It has enriched the prayer lives of countless millions of Christians down the years. Madame Guyon wrote:

'Dear child of God, all your concepts of what God is really like amount to nothing. Do not try to imagine

---

[1] Jeanne Guyon, *Experiencing the depths of Jesus Christ* (Florida: Seedsowers, 1975)

what God is like. Instead, simply believe in His presence. Never try to imagine what God will do. There is no way God will ever fit into your concepts. What then shall you do? Seek to behold Jesus Christ by looking to Him in your inmost being, in your spirit.'

For years I tried to rush into God's presence with a shopping list of petitions instead of taking time to practise the presence of God. Now, I prefer to wait for him to come to me rather than bursting in on him.

I've found the Bible a major source of inspiration for prayer. The psalms are like a prayerbook in themselves, and I've often used them to set my mind to praise and worship. 'Oh how grateful and thankful I am to the Lord because he is so good. I will sing praise to the name of the Lord who is above all lords.' (Ps.7:17 The Living Bible). The psalmists were driven by a mystical passion for God consciousness. Their poetry gives evidence again and again of a sense of abiding communion, and of the reality of a divine presence not confined to time or place.

> Yet I am always with you;
> you hold me by my right hand.
> You guide me with your counsel,
> and afterwards you will take me into glory.
> Whom have I in heaven but you?
> And earth has nothing I desire besides you.
>
> (Ps. 73:23-25).

As I let the words roll around my mind, and meditate on the closeness and love of God, I practise the presence of God and allow him to take me on a journey into his healing, restoring love.

Sometimes I find the words of famous hymns and songs set my mind along the right track for prayer, and

I find their poetry a powerful form of communication with the Lord. Even old hymns which sound corny and old fashioned when sung in church carry a depth of meaning in prayer which I find hard to put into words.

> 'The King of love my shepherd is,
> whose goodness faileth never. . .'

I also find that liturgical prayers can open the door to a new dimension of devotional experience. I've collected a little treasure store of old prayer books over the years which contain pearls of spirituality from a past age. Some of the traditional prayers have a richness of language which is very stimulating, and their very familiarity can be a great comfort in times of stress and strain in my life.

> Protect us through the silent hours of this night, that we who are wearied by the changes and chances of this fleeting world . . . may rest upon your eternal changelessness.

This kind of poetic style is rarely achieved with extempore prayer, in which we are tempted to use the same phrases *ad nauseam* until they lose their meaning.

And more recently I've been discovering how helpful music is as an accompaniment to prayer. I find that music can lead me to the very throne of God.

I never really understood the importance of art in prayer until I attended a Greek Orthodox church one Sunday morning on the island of Lesbos. As the worship continued, the people stood up and walked around looking at the icons on the wall. Many of the worshippers paused before these pictures as they prayed. Of course we're forbidden in the ten commandments to worship graven images, but there's no doubt that art can provide an important focus for prayer.

My favourite place for prayer is in the open air, and I particularly like to pray from a high point overlooking a town. The houses are so small and praying for the community seems somehow more manageable. I find it easier to pray for the world and for those in need from high places like this. I don't know why, I guess it makes Isaiah 40 live for me . . . 'The earth was made by the one who sits on his throne above the earth. . .' It's getting a God perspective!

My favourite style of prayer is to talk to God as I walk. I have several favourite routes which I take, come rain or shine, where I seek God. I have to admit that often I don't feel like going, and that it's sheer willpower that sets me walking.

It takes me ten minutes to focus on the presence of the Lord because there's usually a lot of mental junk that I have to dispose of first. I enjoy the familiarity of my walks, and there's a kind of liturgy in my journey as I divide my track into sections for praise, repentance and personal petition. After twenty minutes or so I find that I have reached that inner silence which enables me to 'practise the presence of God'. When I turn back I feel more able to pray for others, but sometimes the list is so long that I have to ask the Lord to guide me.

The secret of all Christian growth is maintaining this close union with the Lord. I have found that this intimate relationship with him is something which matures with the years. As time has gone by I have come to know him more fully, and to yield my life to him more completely. So, at the heart of my Christian spirituality is a total yielding of all I am and all I have been to him. He's aware of all my personal struggles, failures and flaws . . . and he loves me still. To me, prayer is a sharing of my heart with his heart; the spilling out of my real feelings, unencumbered by what anyone else might say or think. Some of the books of Christian prayer have made the subject far too complex for my taste.

My prayers are often a rag-tag jumble of subjects, and that reflects my normal thought processes, but I'm pretty sure I cover all the ground! Perhaps it's because the Spirit intercedes where my methodology fails!

Over the years of my Christian nurture I was never introduced to the riches of Christian mysticism. Instead, I was schooled in what many would define as the 'evangelical quiet time'. Over recent years, however, I've found this kind of devotion increasingly frustrating. There's something about the culture I live in, the felt needs I have, the personality that is me, and the hunger for reality that pervades my soul . . . that makes fifteen minutes of daily Bible reading notes and a quick 'Our

'I was never introduced to the riches of Christian mysticism.'

Father' insufficient to carry me through the stresses of the day.

Dame Julian of Norwich described in *Revelations of Divine Love* the kind of prayer I'm striving toward; 'When our Lord gives us the grace of revealing himself to our soul, we have what we desire. At that time we are not interested in praying for anything else, because all our attention is fixed on contemplating him.' In a world of growing pressure and pain, I need to discover a form of Christian spirituality which enables me to find the stillness of God's presence in the thick of the action.

I am part of Jesus Christ and he is part of me. When I meet him I ask him to be the centre of all that I am and ever hope to be. For me, the Christian faith is a continuing relationship with Jesus. One of the earliest pieces of advice I received as a young Christian was when a Christian friend pointed me to Paul's letter to the Colossians: 'Since you have accepted Jesus Christ as Lord, live in union with him. Keep your roots deep in him, build your lives on him, and become stronger in your faith. . .'

Your example, Dad, continues to be a guiding inspiration to me.

God bless,
Rob

From: Ronald Frost
To: Rob Frost
CC: Andy Frost; Chris Frost
Subject: Walking with the Lord

Dear Robert,

I think you told me that the visit that three hundred of us made to Israel last year, might not have taken place, if it had not been for something that Christopher had said to you. Apparently you visited him in Leeds university, and when you were parting on the railway station, you said that you were thinking about cancelling the pilgrimage to Israel because of the increasing danger in the region. He asked you why the tour had been arranged in the first place. Your reply was, 'To pray for the peace of Jerusalem, and indeed the whole of the region.'

He then said, 'Well, I should think, in that case, you ought to go all the more!'

You paused before commenting, because the train was just coming into the platform, so he added, 'Dad, if everybody drops out, and you and I go alone, we'll go.' On the strength of that comment you went ahead with the venture, and as we now know, although only three hundred went, it was absolutely right that you should do so.

Of course, there were moments when we were in danger, and times when we were advised not to go to certain places which were usually on a tourist itinerary, but the obvious encouragement that we gave to the people, and the places where we were able to fervently pray for some cessation of the enmity between Jews and Arabs, made us understand that the journey was absolutely right.

With hindsight, it was so right for us to go and it might not have happened if Christopher had not been inspired to say those words of encouragement to you on Leeds railway station. He may not agree, of course, he might have been thinking out the comment and was glad of the opportunity to give it; but it seems to me to be something that was given on the spur of the moment, something that God wanted said, and that he was the vehicle whereby it came. In other words, he was sufficiently spiritually in tune to be God's spokesman in that situation.

Possibly one or the other of you may want to disclaim this and we do have to beware lest pride results from any awareness of divine favour. Nevertheless, that is the way that it seems to me, and there are so many instances in the Bible where God used ordinary people to speak or act for him, because they were spiritually 'tuned in' at the time. I have not been aware of that in my own life very often, but two instances do come to my mind.

The first happened when you were about nine years old. We lived in Stoke-on-Trent at the time, and on summer evenings, always had to play a cricket match in the back garden before you went to bed. We were having a most exciting game when your school friend, Anthony, suddenly opened the back gate and came in. For a few moments he joined in the game, but very soon encouraged you to find another pastime. It was much more exciting to climb onto the garage roof, and make attempts to get from there into the branches of the tree growing from the garden next door.

Realising that my services were no longer needed, as you both descended and turned your attention to tricycles and pedal cars, I just sat on the garden chair, when a thought suddenly came into my mind. 'Go and see the Blakemores.' I had no idea where the thought came from. There was, so far as I could tell, no reason why this family should suddenly flash into my mind. They were connected to the Central Methodist Church in Burslem, although not present every week.

Mr and Mrs Blakemore were both blind, and they had twin boys who could see and were four years old. You can imagine what mischief they could get into, of which their parents were unaware. Well, it was that family that came unsuspectingly into my mind, at that moment, coupled with an apparently clear directive that I was to go and see them. Not that I should include them in my normal pastoral rounds, but that I should, at that moment, drop everything and go. Of course, the arrival of your friend had made my role as playmate obsolete, and I knew that mother would call you in when it was bed time. I jumped into the car, and drove to Sneyd Green where the Blakemores lived.

When I rang the door bell, I knew there was something wrong, for I could hear lots of shouting inside, as someone was trying to instruct one of the twins to open the door, and there was much noise of him climbing up to reach the lock.

Once admitted, I made my way into the living room, where the father said, 'Thank goodness you've come', and the mother said, 'How did you know to come?' Those were the days when very few homes had a telephone, so they could not think by what kind of telepathy I had appeared to meet their need.

There was blood all over the place. The mother was too weak to get out of the armchair, the father was holding a blood soaked towel to his head and the twin who had not opened the door was sitting on the floor crying. It did not, in fact take many minutes to restore order, to stop the bleeding and to get the wounds bandaged. The fact that the adults could not see what was going on had added to the sense of drama, and been responsible for the resulting chaos. Soon, however, I was able to hear what had happened. The mother had been cutting a loaf for the family's tea, (cut loaves were a novelty in those days and not normally used by poorer families, because they were more expensive.) The knife had slipped and she had cut her hand.

She had instructed the twins to get the first-aid kit out of the built in cupboard by the fire-place. One of them had climbed up onto the arm of the armchair, but toppled over, and cut his knee on the edge of the fender. (What's a fender? It's a metal surround that keeps the ashes from an open coal fire from getting out onto the floor covering of the rest of the room. Most houses were heated by burning coal in a grate in those days.)

The mother had shouted to the boy that the first-aid box was not in the upper part of the cupboard, but on the lower shelf. It was the kind of cupboard that had one set of doors for the top shelves, and another set of doors for the lower shelves. When the little boy had climbed up, he had left the upper doors open, but of course the father could not see this. Consequently when he had got the first-aid box out, and then stood up to take it to his wife, his head had hit the open upper door, and cut his scalp.

To a sighted family this would not have been a very great crisis, but to the Blakemores to have three members all with bleeding wounds at the same time meant the need of outside help. They had no way of summoning this. I don't even know if they said a prayer, but God knew their predicament, and I suppose that I must have been spiritually in tune just at that time.

The other occasion, when I believe I had a clear message from God was one which, to my shame, I did not obey. I used the name Blakemore for my first illustration, although I really cannot remember the name of the family but know that the details are correct. For my next example, I remember the name of the boy quite clearly, but will change it, as some people who read this may still know him. The event occurred when I was Superintendent minister of the Plymouth Central Hall.

Our skiffle group had been invited to play in the Royal Albert Hall in London, for the annual display of the Methodist Association of Youth Clubs, on the same weekend as the Sunday school anniversary. It was agreed that the Wesley deaconess would take all the members of the youth club on the night coach to London, and that they would assemble at the coach station.

On the Friday evening, I stationed myself with about half a dozen other men from the church, in order to put up the platform that entirely covered the communion area, and provided seating for the couple of hundred children who augmented the choir for such a festival. It was heavy work, and I had crawled underneath the planks, to secure them with nuts and bolts, using the various tools that had been provided. As I lay there, well aware that there were other men far more used to handling tools than I was, the thought suddenly came into my mind, 'You ought to go and call for Leon Rilston.'

Leon Rilston was a member of the youth club from a broken home. There was not so much understanding of what effect this could have on teenage behaviour in those days, and the result was that he was labelled as a criminal, had been before the magistrates on several occasions, and had been put under the care of the local authority. Special arrangements had been made for him to be absent from the children's home for the weekend, so that he could experience the trip to London with the others.

As I lay under the incomplete stage, I thought, 'Supposing he forgets the details of the arrangement. Supposing he is so used to the regimented regime that he can't just walk out. Supposing he misses the bus and doesn't get to the coach station in time. Supposing. . .' Then the apparent command came, 'There are plenty of men who can put this platform up, and they're much more able to do it than you. You go and collect Leon, then there'll be no doubt about his having the fantastic week-end in London.'

I know now that it was a message from God, but in my pride, I said to myself, 'I want the other men of the church to think that I am a real man, that I can carry heavy planks, and use tools as well as they can. If I go and collect Leon, they will think that I am shirking manual work.' So I didn't go.

At midnight on Sunday the telephone rang. It was the children's home. They had given permission for Leon to be away for the week-end. They had read the correspondence from the church which said that he would be back by 10 o'clock on Sunday. It was now midnight and he hadn't arrived. A frantic phone call to the Deaconess revealed that he had never arrived at the coach station. The party had had a marvellous week-end, but Leon had not been with them.

Two days later he was found by the police. Once he had left his children's home there was no one to make sure that he went where he was supposed to go. He had used his short liberty to meet up with some of his old mates, they had taken a small motor launch, travelled to another Devon coastal town and generally made a nuisance of themselves until the police had apprehended them.

How I have regretted not obeying that word from the Lord, because I wanted the men of the Church to think well of me. Since then I have not consciously been aware of such a divine directive.

Looking back, however, I am not sure that that means that I am never motivated by spirituality. Indeed the older I get, the more it seems to me that my life is guided by God, and that things that might appear quite ordinary are in fact happening because they are within the divine plan.

When I was secretary of the Chester and Stoke-on-Trent district of the Methodist church, an old minister, the Reverend Arthur Utton, was the chairman. He didn't drive, so I spent many hours in his company travelling everywhere between Holyhead in the north and Stone in Staffordshire in the south! I didn't really understand then what he often said, but I'm beginning to comprehend it more and more. 'The older I get,' he said, 'the less I say my prayers, but the more I pray.'

Of course, I do still have a prayer and Bible reading time on waking and before retiring, but they are not as long as they once were. However, I do find myself talking to God at every touch and turn of life. Then it doesn't seem so much like me talking, but rather having a conversation, and in that sense, I'm quite sure that I get to know what God wants me to do. Often that message is, 'Don't get so het up about things. You missed that train, but don't worry, there'll be another.' 'Be still and know that I am God.'

I hope this is helpful,

Dad

From: Andy Frost
To: Rob Frost
CC: Ronald Frost; Chris Frost
Subject: Walking with the Lord

Dear Dad,

Walking with the Lord is all about intimacy. But what is intimacy?

With loneliness rife in today's society, with casual sex on the increase and with family breakdown becoming ever prevalent, society seems to have lost this idea of 'imtimate relationship'. The advertisers use it to sell us a product; it is the author's cunning device to gain our affinity with a character, and the director's technique for selling a film . . . it is intimacy that all of us long for.

Rarely are the ideas of intimacy and God closely connected. Though we may call our faith 'relationship', too often the relationship becomes ten minutes of time spent staring blankly at a verse in Leviticus. We teach our children that prayer is like a telephone, yet many of us talk through our shopping lists of requests without ever listening. When God speaks we limit the ways we hear according to the ways we have always known, the trappings of tradition and culture. Is this intimacy? Is this depth? Is this even a real relationship?

If we want to become a spiritual church, intimacy with God is vital. If we do not know the Father's heart, if we are not able to change and adapt areas of our life that he intimately reveals, if we do not know his direction . . . how can we possibly become people of God? An intimate relationship with God is key. Moses was intimate with God at the burning bush; Samuel was awoken as he heard God speak intimately; Isaiah was personally commissioned in an intimate encounter; and

Stephen had an intimacy with his heavenly Father as he became the first Christian martyr.

Perhaps my favourite expression in the Bible is 'Noah walked with God'. I picture this Simpson-esque idea of long bearded Noah walking and talking with the Lord. This is what I desire . . .

Yet somehow we seem to have lost this intimacy with God that is so biblically consistent, recurring in generation after generation. Occasionally we glimpse the breadcrumbs of intimacy. Yet we mistakenly believe that they are the loaves that God wants to give us. We are continually short-changed and rob ourselves of what God has in store for us. Fear, guilt, and a lack of expectancy are among the culprits that hold back generation from the fruition of intimacy that God wants us to have.

Even the breadcrumbs of intimacy are the exception rather than a current part of our lives. Intimacy with God remains out of reach unless we are surrounded by an array of greens and blues as we survey his creation from a mountaintop, or unless we are in a hyped setting where the worship band is 'anointed'. Though there are definite highs and lows along our journey, intimacy should remain constant, whether we are straining to meet a deadline late on a Friday sat at our desk; or whether we are stewing in a traffic jam. Intimacy with God should be continual.

As a teenager, I longed for intimacy. And it was this 'walking with God' theology that was lacking in the church setting. Singing songs and reading the Bible was all very nice, but without intimacy with God, it was meaningless. It led to a personal search for intimacy in relationships with others, intimacy with women. The desire of my heart was a deep spiritual intimacy that many of my peers were searching for, too. The established church failed to reveal such depth, yet secular culture seemed to offer no answers either.

I had constructed a distorted view of God. He was Creator; the omnipotent God; but I had failed to see the true intimacy of God. This appears to be a common misconception deeply embedded within our society. As I hit fifteen the idea of God as 'father' and 'friend' was quickly disappearing into the abyss. I continued to believe that God existed but I believed that he was up in heaven somewhere and that he was not really a God that wanted too much to do with me personally. He was probably pretty busy, and intimacy with a grunge obsessed A-level kid. He had the AIDS epidemic and the starving in Africa to deal with was not foremost on his agenda. He didn't really want to hear from me – did He?

I think that when we study the magnitude and the breadth of God, we are truly humbled. This is a healthy exercise as long as we maintain our understanding of the other side of God's character. We must remember that God is relational and that he cares for each of us. His heart's desire is intimacy with us. He desires it so much that he sent his own Son down to earth to enter the world as a man in order to have affinity with mankind. He was even willing to send his Son to die on a cross that our iniquity could be taken away and the path to a relationship with him opened up. He wants us to share our lives with him.

When we settle down to our quiet times, this looming picture of the all-powerful God can disfigure our vision of the relational Father (Mt. 7). We must remember the complete personality of God when coming into his presence. If we expect to merely focus on the vastness of God without recognising his personal side, we will not expect God to want to speak to us. If we do not expect God to speak to us, how will we ever hear his voice? As I have come to understand that God does want intimacy with me personally, beyond five minutes spent in prayer, I began to expect to hear him. I began striving for intimacy with him. Sometimes I was able to hear him clearly, yet at other times his voice became distant and quiet. This experience has changed my whole understanding of prayer. But I've still much to learn.

Always searching for greater depth,
Andy

From: Chris Frost
To: Rob Frost
CC: Ronald Frost; Andy Frost;
Subject: Walking with the Lord

Dear Dad,

I reckon the biggest thing that gets on my nerves is competitive Christianity and I'll put my hands up and say I'm probably one of the worst culprits. Competitive Christianity is at its worse when we hold our heads high on a Sunday morning because we haven't slipped up that week or when we brag about the hours of deep intercession we've just had. Wasn't it Jesus who preached it's what's on the inside that matters? We make such a big show with an outward form of religion that we forget that Jesus wants to transform us from the inside.

One of the strongest influences on my life is a guy called Tim. He is so humble, so servant hearted, kind and compassionate, oh, and he swears. And he swears because he wants God to change his heart rather than rushing ahead of him to fit in nicely on a Sunday morning. Now I'm not saying that I'm a great fan of swearing but I do hate religious attitudes; ones that pick up on everyone elses' specks of sawdust and completely miss the planks of wood in their own eyes. So I think this is where my spirituality starts; on the inside, so I guess its going to be hard to try and explain it.

The Christian culture which has emerged is often rather damaging: it can be so inward looking, so cliquey and is often sickly and cheesy. Much like the world outside the church, we have often sought to idolise any human we can get our hands on. So often at a church gathering you'll hear something like: 'Do you know that

so and so prays for x hours a day . . .' Now there's nothing wrong in looking to heroes of the faith for inspiration but so often young Christians can compare their
seeming 'little' to others and either give up or idolise
them. I think on my journey I've come to realise that no
matter how hard I try, I'm not ready for some of the hard
core spiritual acts that you read about in books. Not that
I'm going to sit back on a spiritual deckchair and watch
the world go by but a journey is a journey. I'm going to
keep pressing on to the end, realising more and more
how pathetic I am and how great God is. And I know
that it's a hunger for God that will keep me on the move:
I want to see his face!

I think we all meet God in different ways at different
times. I think a lot of my spirituality is released and
received around other people: I'd much rather pray with
other people than on my own and I used to feel so guilty
about this but now I know that it's the way that God has
wired me, so it must be okay. As I focus my energy on
the things I like doing, I find everything else seems to
play 'catch-up'. I know after a long worship session I can
be so hungry for God's word.

I think my spiritual life is just about as messy as my
room, which according to mum 'looks like a bomb has
hit it.' I can remember wanting to have a perfect plan to
cover all my needs but it never seemed to come. Now I
realise that every day is a new day; I have new needs
and constraints in it. So I've started to stylise my spiritual time appropriately and it's that diversity which
keeps me hooked to my Heavenly Father. I know my
girlfriend Jo wouldn't be best pleased if we only spent
time together for an hour a day, sitting in the same place
at the same time: the relationship would run so dry! I
think one of the most intimate times I've had with Jesus
was when I built a sandcastle on Fistral beach with him.

After all wasn't it Jesus who walked, ate, laughed and played with his disciples? I don't feel as if I do a great job of abiding in Christ but I'd like to say I'm all right at being real with him. I think the band Nirvana expressed it best in the satirical lyrics: 'Come as you are, as a friend, as I want you to be.'

Hungry for more,
Chris

From: Rob Frost
To: Ronald Frost
CC: Andy Frost; Chris Frost;
Subject: Walking with the Lord

Dear Dad, Andy and Chris,

I was glad that you shared your two examples of hearing God, Dad. They are an indication of true spirituality,
of being in tune with God's will! I've been aware of a
similar sense of connection in my own life, though only
rarely.

On one very snowy day in Yorkshire, when I was first
a Methodist minister, I had been out visiting the shut-ins
and the sick. I was very tired, and the snow was cascad-
ing down as the car slithered homeward. Just then, I had
an overwhelming sense that I must visit the Town
Mayor, who attended our chapel.

I turned the car round and drove up the steep hill
towards his house. We had a wonderful time of fellowship, laughter, sharing and prayer. Later that
night his wife phoned to say that he had died, very
suddenly, of a heart attack just a few hours after I had
left.

I always felt that visiting that man was part of
God's agenda, rather than my own. I'm sure that
when we're in tune, we really do his will rather than
ours, and I guess we'll only know just how much of
his agenda we completed when we meet him face to
face!

I guess it's this kind of relationship with Jesus
which you describe as intimacy, Andy; a depth of
relationship which transcends saying our prayers. It's
about the whole of life. As you so rightly say, Chris,
it's about building sandcastles and being hooked to

the Father. We're all at different stages on the same journey.

God bless,
Rob

9

Looking to the Future

From: Rob Frost
To: Ronald Frost
CC: Andy Frost; Chris Frost
Subject: Looking to the Future

Dear Dad, Andy and Chris,

I don't feel particularly old, but now I've hit my fifties I do have more thoughts about my mortality. A sense of the brevity of life does come more often than when I was your age, Andy and Chris! Several of my contemporaries have already died, and others are eagerly looking forward to retirement.

I am writing this as I approach another birthday, and I've been asking myself . . . what's the bottom line of my life? I generally spend some time around my birthday reflecting on my life and on what I've done over the last year. A kind of profit-loss equation drawn from the experience of the last twelve months. How can one measure one's progress? Am I a success or a failure? Have I done well, or could I do better? I see the popular heroes of our age paraded before me on TV screens and magazine covers and try to exorcise a tinge of jealousy.

What's the latest news of Bill Gates, Richard Branson, Rupert Murdoch or David Beckham? And do I really care? And if, like them, I could have anything money could buy would it make me happy, or simply make me hunger for more? With their success I'd get more choice . . . but would choosing then become a stressful preoccupation. There would be more friends . . . but would they be the kind of friends who would stand beside me through thick and thin? With their money I'd have more possessions . . . but maybe my personal security would be a living nightmare. So, as I look at the bottom line of my personal account, maybe there are advantages in being Mr Ordinary, after all.

To be honest, I sometimes feel a bit of a failure. In this world's terms I really haven't made it big time. I guess there comes a time in all of our lives when each of us has to face the fact that we haven't done all we'd hoped to do, or found the success that others have seemingly achieved so effortlessly.

Money? I've not got much and there's always a shortage of cash, but if there wasn't, my section of the flock might be asking some awkward questions. Fame? Hardly. My latest preach isn't going to make the TV news and my latest article for *Christianity & Renewal* magazine won't get quoted on *Panorama*. Power? Nothing to speak of. I might get to sway the vote at a Methodist Synod or give a seminar at Spring Harvest, but it'll hardly make the government quake.

I sense there are a lot of us around; ordinary people who would be glad of a taste of fame, even for fifteen minutes. Yet we live our days making the best of what we've got and learning to accept who we've become. Perhaps this feeling is accentuated in mid-life, when the

track ahead seems shorter than the road already travelled. The stark truth is that many mountains I once
dreamed of climbing remain unscaled, and many ambitions still remain unfulfilled.

Which brings me back to my birthday, and my return
to familiar territory. For again and again across the years
of my discipleship I've become aware of God's bottom
line. For, indisputably, he has one. God has his own
alternative ways of measuring success or failure. And I
suspect that his league-tables are rather different from
my own. In my more reflective moments I can sense him
measuring my life. My plans might seem exciting to me,
but they're useless unless they've got his nod of
approval. My performance might seem outstanding, but
it's hollow if my motives are wrong. My management
might seem tightly efficient, but it's flawed if it isn't
ultimately fully accountable to him. So, if I want to

**'My performance might seem outstanding – but it's
hollow if my motives are wrong.'**

satisfy God's bottom line I need to place my 'doing' in the context of his 'being'.

God's bottom line isn't about profit and loss. It's about right and wrong, love and hate, good and bad, truth and falsehood, integrity and double-dealing. God's bottom line isn't measured by success . . . it's about obedience, and faithfulness, and about living a life completely given over to him. There is a bottom line more precious than ISAs, gilts, pension funds and deposit accounts. It's something called wisdom. And it's something that is more valuable than the glitter of a success dominated society. It's only his wisdom that can help this birthday boy avoid evil, guard his soul, live humbly, trust him, discern right, speak intelligently . . . and recognise that there's more to life than worldly success. God's bottom line is revealed when we stand before Jesus at the end of time and hear him ask, 'Well?' So . . . a toast to my birthday . . . and the simple question that lies at the heart of my understanding of destiny . . . what's the bottom line of my life?

Pilgrim's Progress is a book all about journeys. The journey of one man from the City of Destruction to the City of Heaven. The journey of Faithful and Hopeful who accompany him at difficult times on the road of life. The journey of countless other characters, most of whom are travelling in the wrong direction . . . or who are hopelessly lost along the road of life. Yet the driving force of the drama is that Christian is making a journey and that he knows his ultimate destination. He knows where he's heading and the sustaining hope of reaching the Eternal City is what carries him along the painful path of his journey.

The book is a reflection of John Bunyan's own seventeenth century journey. Many of his own adventures, struggles and sufferings are mirrored in the story. He grew up in poverty, the son of a tinsmith. He joined the army, and when a friend replaced him on guard duty one night, this friend was killed. Bunyan came into a deep awareness of his own sin and failure, and it was a great revelation to him that the grace of Jesus was sufficient, even for him. He was always a rebel, and his commitment to non-conformity and to preaching this gospel of grace led to a twelve year prison sentence in Bedford gaol. Yet it was his destination which kept Bunyan faithful to the journey. The promise of the heavenly kingdom, the City of Light, and the everlasting love of Jesus Christ.

My own life is more than a diary of appointments, a list of jobs to do, or a sequence of difficult meetings to attend. My life is a pilgrimage, and I am on my way to a destination. And the route I take today determines which way I'm headed eternally. So this, as I look to the future, is my destiny. My life is a journey, and if I really want to travel this journey with Jesus it will demand everything.

God bless,
Rob

From: Ronald Frost
To: Rob Frost
CC: Andy Frost; Chris Frost
Subject: Looking to the Future

Dear Robert,

I did not want to retire after forty-nine years as a Methodist minister in September 1994, within a few weeks of my seventy-fourth birthday. It would have been nice to have completed my half century; I was in perfectly good health. As far as I could tell everything was going well within the North and Central London Mission, where the next year would hold the Diamond Jubilee celebration of the Archway Central Hall and where I had been privileged to serve for the past nine years.

The composition of the mission committee that had to decide whether I continued in post or not, required that I got 8.25 votes of those voting. In fact I only obtained 8 votes, so in spite of many protests from the ordinary church members, I had to go. I was disappointed, but as in everything else during my life, I have now proved another nine years later, that 'All things work together for good to them that love God, and to those who are called according to his purpose.'

One of the reasons why I wanted to stay 'in post' was because housing an additional member of the Circuit staff meant that I had long since moved out of the beautiful manse in Muswell Hill and come to live in what was built as the caretaker's flat at the top of the Central Hall building. This suited my dog Susie and I admirably. It was possible to step out onto the flat roof and have a bird's eye view of the immediate locality and the amazing London sky-line. I was reluctant to leave this. I loved living at the hub of such a busy and diverse community, with the traffic perpetually swirling round the Archway roundabout, twenty-four hours a day.

Nevertheless I had to go, and wondered where the Methodist Ministers' Housing Society (a charity specially set up to house Methodist ministers and their families when they retire) would be able to find me a place. I desperately wanted to stay in North London, but realised that there were very few such places because property in London was so very expensive. I was given the choice of a house in Ruislip and a basement flat in Kensal Rise, when suddenly a beautiful house in East Finchley became available. Nothing could have been better from my point of view, and I accepted it without delay.

There were five reasons why I wanted to stay in North London. First, having lived there since 1977, I had developed many friendships, and knew that if in my declining years I needed practical help, there would be many lovely people who would be on hand. Then I knew that the Circuits in the area found it hard to get preachers for all their services every Sunday, and I felt that I could be of use continuing a ministry leading worship in a variety of churches.

It was with some trepidation that I agreed to continue as the Captain of the 10th London Boys' Brigade Company that met at the Central Hall, because I did not want to cause any embarrassment or difficulty for my successor. However, I could see that there was no obvious person who could take over from me, so agreed to go to the week-day meetings but not the Sunday services until he had had time to establish himself.

Another reason why I wanted to stay in North London was that, most surprisingly and without any seeking on my part, I had started to be recognised as a private tutor. I suppose it started when a teenager who had been converted during my Birmingham ministry had expressed a desire to become a Methodist minister, but had not passed the necessary school examinations. He used to visit me in my early years in London, so that I could prepare him for 'A' level English, Maths and Religious Knowledge. This was a purely private arrangement that re-introduced me to the academic standards required for university entrance.

Soon after my wife died, however, I got a telephone call from the principal of the technical college in Tottenham, who asked if I could help three of his students who wanted to take Religious Knowledge at 'A' level. I could not see how he could possibly have heard of my tutoring the young man from Birmingham (who became the Reverend David Rigby, and who sadly died only a few years after his ordination) so I told him that I did not think that I was really qualified to help him.

He said, 'I badly need your help. The boilers have all gone wrong at the college, and these three young men have an examination in December. We are not allowed to use our classrooms unheated, so we need to get them taught off of our premises. I thought that if you could teach them in your house, my problem would be solved.'

I told him that there would be no problem with the three young men coming to my house for several hours each week, but that I did not think I had the ability to be a tutor. My degree had been obtained in 1952, and I had spent my life preaching, not teaching. The principal continued to pressurise me, however, and he said, 'I have just come off the phone from the Methodist Headquarters and they tell me that you are one of their official tutors, and they assure me that you are a tutor in Bible Studies.'

Again I told him that I was not, but he seemed so desperate that I asked him to give me the telephone number that he had rung and then perhaps I could find out with whom I was being confused. I made the phone call and was told, 'But Mr. Frost, when you first got your degree you were a tutor in Bible Studies for the correspondence courses of the Methodist study centre, and your name is still on our books.'

I hadn't had time to pursue my association with the Methodist study centre for twenty years, indeed I did not know that it was still in existence, but I could then see how it was that the principal had obtained his information. I had, of course, got all the notes that I had used to help David Rigby, so thought that I probably could help the students with their pending examinations. So I phoned the principal back, and for the next six weeks the three young men came for tuition three mornings a week. One was a Jew, one was a Hindu and one was a Roman Catholic.

It was a wonderful experience and was one of the ways, I think, that God had planned for me to come to terms with the recent death of my dear wife. I fear that sometimes the answering of their questions made it more like a Methodist class meeting than a tutorial group. To study Isaiah with a Jew; to explain the crucifixion and resurrection to a Hindu, and to speak of Grace in the Epistle to the Romans to a Roman Catholic, were absolute gifts to a Methodist preacher! The academic side must have been present, however, because each of them ultimately phoned to say that he had passed.

It was about six months later that the Hindu phoned me and said that his sister's family were in difficulty. They spoke Gujarati at home and in consequence the headmistress of the school that his niece attended would not let her take O level English; she would have to take the CSE examination instead. The family were quite sure that the girl could manage the higher grade, but the headmistress would not think of it. He said that as I had helped him so much with his Religious Knowledge, he felt sure that I could help this girl with her English. To cut a long story short, I did and she got an A grade, taking 'O' level externally.

Everything developed from there. I never advertised: one satisfied family told another, so that by the time retirement came I was spending every early evening, between afternoon pastoral visiting time and evening meeting time acting as a private tutor to teenagers and children whose parents thought that they needed extra help. Moreover, I had been introduced to the American University in London who were looking for a tutor who could help overseas students with their English. So it was that when retirement came, I had built up quite a network of people who thought that I could help them with their studies. This, then, was another reason why I wanted to stay in North London when retirement came.

My fifth reason was that one morning the telephone rang and the Secretary of the National United Temperance Council introduced himself to me. He said that he had heard of the way that I had upheld the cause of total abstinence, in spite of it being a rather unpopular feature in our current national life. I was surprised that my efforts in that direction should have been noticed at such a high level, and even more astonished, when, because of what he had heard, he said that the Council had recently met and had unanimously expressed the wish that I should become their national chairman.

I accepted the voluntary position because I signed the pledge in the Band of Hope when I was about eight years old, and by God's grace have, so far as I know, never broken it. Whilst being a Circuit Superintendent, however, the amount of time that I could give to the position was extremely limited and I thought that in retirement I could be much more effective. I knew that it would be far easier to do this if I lived in the capital city.

Two Methodist ministers from the past who have had a great influence on my life are Dr. Scott Lidgett and Dr. E. Benson Perkins. Each of them wrote an autobiography. Lidgett's was called *My Guided Life*, and Perkins' was called *So Appointed*. The nine years that I have so far spent in retirement have helped me to understand those titles, for it seems to me that there is without any doubt a loving heavenly Father who has been leading me into the future.

All the five reasons for my wanting to stay in London have been fulfilled, and I constantly want to sing,

> I'll bless the Hand the guided,
> I'll praise the Heart that planned

'Most of the boys came from an Afro-Caribbean background.'

My friendships have become even more meaningful and there are few Sundays when I am not planned somewhere or another.

The 10th London Boys' Brigade Company has gone from strength to strength. This has been shown by the fact that three young men have become 'Queensmen', ten were invited to Windsor Castle for the Brigade's Centenary Royal Review; six were given the honour of marching in the Queen's Jubilee procession, and twelve have recently taken part in the London District Band's tour of the Netherlands to celebrate that nation's commemoration and liberation days.

As if to counterbalance the fact that in 1935 my school friend and I were so excited to go and hear twelve black people sing, today in 2003 out of the present forty members of the 10th London Company of the Boy's Brigade, only four (two boys and two officers –

Ronald Frost receives the OBE at Buckingham Palace.

including myself) are white! Most of the boys and the other two officers are from an Afro-Caribbean background.

The fact that Her Majesty bestowed upon me the honour of becoming an Officer of the Order of the British Empire because of my involvement in youth work is perhaps an indication that I was meant to remain in London after I had officially retired. I was most surprised that she had ever heard of me, or the things that I had been doing, but I gratefully received her award, because I felt that our family's service in the very poorest parts of London, stretching back for over a century to the days of Grandfather Frost and Great Grandfather Newman, had been rendered selflessly, without thought of reward, but purely because those doing it felt that they were following Jesus.

So far as the teaching is concerned there are now some twenty-five families who show confidence in me and welcome me into their homes to assist in the education of their children. Since these come from a variety of ethnic backgrounds with diverse cultures and religions, I feel greatly privileged when I find myself continuing a kind of pastoral ministry, as they feel able to share with me their hopes and fears, their delights and frustrations. Similarly, being asked to help potential university students from other countries to become sufficiently fluent in English, so that they can pursue their courses in this country, has given me the opportunity of sorting out all kinds of problems that occur when young people are in strange surroundings, far from their families and native lands.

My involvement in the Temperance Movement has also demonstrated that it was right for me to stay in London, because I have found myself called to Parliamentary Committees to comment upon proposed licensing law. In addition to this, of course, there has been the ever present awareness of my closely knit family, always prepared to help, always available to support, always on hand to encourage. This has not only applied to the son and grandsons with whom I have shared this correspondence, but my dear sister, Rita, and my marvellous daughter-in-law, Jacqui.

I am not naive enough to think that everything will essentially continue with such equanimity. There may yet be problems and difficulties ahead, weaknesses, disappointments, and limitations in declining powers, but I have experienced so much of God's goodness, that I can sing with confidence with Joseph Hart,

> I'll praise Him for all that is past,
> And trust Him for all that's to come.

That trusting for all that's to come includes for me the time when time shall be no more – eternity. I understand that the new Millennium was welcomed in Australia by one huge illuminated word that stretched the whole length of Sydney Harbour Bridge. Some say that it was so brilliant that it could even be seen in New Zealand! The one word was Eternity.

I heard some intellectuals discussing it on Radio Four, and it was said that the sign was not only welcoming the twenty-first century, but was also advertising an opera that had been specially written for the period by Jonathan Miller entitled *The Eternity Man*. Those taking part in the discussion tried to find out the identity of *The Eternity Man*, and concluded that Jonathan Miller never revealed it. It was for each person to decide for themselves.

Well, so far as I am concerned, for Ronald William Frost, 'The Eternity Man' is and was and ever will be Jesus, God Incarnate. 'For' as St Paul wrote in the eighth chapter of the Epistle to the Romans, 'I am persuaded that neither death, nor life, nor angels, nor principalities, nor powers, nor things present, nor things to come, nor height nor depth, nor any other creature shall be able to separate us from the love of God, which is in Christ Jesus our Lord.'

With much love
'Boss'

(I sign off with the nickname our family has adopted for me from the children at our Alvechurch summer camp).

From: Andy Frost
To: Rob Frost
CC: Ronald Frost; Chris Frost
Subject: Looking to the Future

Dear Dad,

When one day I look back at my life, more than being able to look back at lists of achievements, I want to be able to look back at my journey towards God. I have been able to say that like a lump of clay I want to be broken, moulded and shaped into a man of God. As I write this prayer from my heart, a nervous shudder runs down my spine as I wonder if I know exactly what I am asking for.

As I journey towards holiness, the further I journey, the more I realise that I have so far to go to reach the perfection of Christ. I will never arrive at a destination where I can say I have attained and become all that I can. There is always a further milestone, another bend on the path. I do not write as one who has seen the map but as one who has travelled over some of the mountain peaks and into some of the valleys. I wish to encourage my fellow travellers, identifying some of the forks in the path that one must cross once, twice or maybe a thousand times; forks in the road where we must choose either the easy route or God's route.

Paul writes, 'Therefore I do not run like a man running aimlessly; I do not fight like a man beating the air. No, I beat my body and make it my slave so that after I have preached to others, I myself will not be disqualified from the prize.' The journey to becoming a man of God is both consuming and excruciating. It involves the sincerest discipline, the utmost focus; and as we seek God's face, we only pray that one day we might be called 'faithful servant.'

Britain is in a spiritual mess – we live in a society devoid of meaning where truth is relative and everyone is trying to live by their own rulebook. The present age is not dissimilar to the time when the book of Judges in the Old Testament was written. 'In those days Israel had no king; everyone did as he saw fit' (17:6). In this society today there is no king. Though many still believe in some kind of a higher being, few know his name and fewer still follow his decrees. With no one to be responsible to, people have lost their moral and ethical code. People merely do what appears right according to their own perceptions. They no longer have a truth to adhere to. They live for themselves. They hide their selfish perversions with smooth words. They hide their highly sexualised and depraved ways of living with terminology, such as 'alternative lifestyles'. The world around us looks dark.

It was the same in the book of Judges – darkness prevailed. The Israelites had failed to follow God's command to wipe out the enemies from the land. They then intermarried and were lured into idolatry. In the same way, the church today has lacked obedience. Though it is meant to be the Bride of Christ (Rev. 19:7), it has lusted after the things of this world; has failed to be obedient; and has fallen into mediocrity. (Rather than being a beautiful virgin dressed in white, she looks more like a whore walking up the aisle in stockings and suspenders!)

Yet I believe the times are changing and as in the book of Judges, God is going to call up leaders to bring the people back to the one and only living God. Many of the judges had great flaws, like Jephthah who made a foolish vow that led to the death of his daughter (11:31); and Samson who was frequently controlled by his sensual desires (16:15-20). . . . but they were still able to accomplish great things through God's grace. It was their submission to God that enabled them to be utilised so powerfully. The way that biblical characters are remembered is always interesting. There are countless genealogies and few characters stand out. Jabez is one of the characters who is actually remembered as more than just the son of someone and the father of someone else. He is recorded as a man with a prayer for wider territories, a man who desired more from God.

I hope that during my time on earth I will use the limited number of years wisely. I hope that I will be remembered as more than the son of Rob Frost and perhaps the father of another Frost! I pray that I will be remembered as a Jesus revolutionary – someone passionate for God and his ways. We can no longer let ourselves be consumed with self-pity. Instead we must cast the past aside and break the curse of what has gone before. Becoming men and women of God is about becoming a spiritual warrior securely founded in God's truth. We should no longer be weak because within each of us there is unbridled strength. We are called to be meek not weak. It is not so much about what we do but about who we are. Psalm 24, verse 3 to 6 reads. .

'I hope I will use the limited years wisely.' (Andy on mission in Brazil).

Who may ascend the hill of the Lord?
Who may stand in his holy place?
He who has clean hands and a pure heart,
Who does not lift up his soul to an idol
Or swear by what is false.
He will receive blessing from the Lord
And vindication from God his Saviour.
Such is the generation of those who seek him,
Who seek your face, O God of Jacob

If we truly want to be men and women of God we must start by seeking his face. The story of Jacob wrestling with God illustrates how we must struggle to discover God's blessings. Jacob wrestled all night and would not let the man go until he had received the blessing. We must have this same desire to seek God's face if we truly want to be transformed.

One of the biggest issues that our generation has to deal with is apathy. Too often we are not willing to put the effort into seeking God's face and so, in due course, we do not receive the blessings that he wants to bestow on us. When our society says that we are worthless and the church establishment is unwilling to listen to us, we as a generation have too often shied away and missed out.

The challenge ahead of us is great and there are many attractive paths that could lead us away from the true path. We must keep surrendering. We must keep obeying. Are we really willing to lay down all and take up the cross. In the words of Delirious? 'Do we really want to be history makers?'

Forever challenged,
Andy

From: Chris Frost
To: Rob Frost
CC: Ronald Frost; Andy Frost;
Subject: Looking to the Future

Dear Dad,

Throughout my Christian life I've had sleepless nights tossing the idea in my mind that this is going to be the generation that God uses to see the Kingdom of Heaven break out like never before! Is this vain of me: is it just a reflection of the proud postmodern world that we live in?

I look around my Christian Union at Leeds university and am overwhelmed by the passion for Jesus among the Christians, that seems to overcome any differences between us. It seems to be a model for the future and

'Curse the day I swap my cross for a pair of slippers.'
(Chris on mission in Palestine).

tells me that maybe my dreams for this nation are obtainable and maybe God will surprise us all again. But then you turn around and tell me that that passion will soon deflate into the welcoming arms of 'life', a place so well defined by the cult classic film *Trainspotting*:

> Choose Life. Choose a job. Choose a career. Choose a family. Choose a big television. Choose washing machines, cars, compact disc players and electrical tin openers. Choose leisurewear and matching luggage. Choose a three-piece suite on higher purchase and a range of fabrics. Choose DIY wondering who you are on a Sunday morning. Choose your future. Choose life . . . (Irvine Welsh: *Trainspotting*).

Curse the day that I swap my cross for a pair of slippers, I'm not going to! I want to see Jesus transforming lives like he has mine, no matter what the cost.

Did you used to think the same when you were a youth? Am I being unwise in expecting more of God? Should I stick to strategic mission rather than crying out to God to heal our land?

I read about John and Charles Wesley leading thousands to Christ and my heart seems to cry 'Oh God, that you would restore these works in this time.' I'm believing God for a great revival along the lines that Smith Wigglesworth, the famous healing evangelist, prophesied on 12th of March 1947[1]:

> During the next few decades there will be two distinct moves of the Holy Spirit across the Church in Great Britain. The first move will affect every church that is

---

[1] Robert Liardon, *Smith Wigglesworth* (Oklahoma: Albury Publishing, 1996)

open to receive it and will be characterized by a restoration of the baptism and gifts of the Holy Spirit. The second move of the Holy Spirit will result in people leaving historic churches and planting new churches.

In the duration of each of these moves, the people who are involved will say 'This is the great revival.' But the Lord says 'No, neither is the great revival but both are steps towards it.'

When the new church phase is on the wane, there will be evidence in the churches of something that has not been seen before: a coming together of those with an emphasis on the Word and those with an emphasis on the Spirit. When the Word and the Spirit come together, there will be the biggest movement of the Holy Spirit that the nation, and indeed the world, has ever seen. It will mark the beginning of a revival that will eclipse anything that has been witnessed within these shores, even the Wesleyan and the Welsh revivals of former years. The outpouring of God's Spirit will flow over from the UK to the mainland of Europe, and from there will begin a missionary move to the ends of the earth.

And why not our nation, and why not for such a time as this? I know I need to be committed to the small for the big to come. After all that's what Jesus did, but I'm fed up with a social gospel with no power and a comfortable Jesus that says 'you're fine where you are'. I want to see the possessed released, the lame healed, the hungry fed and the lost saved: I want the lion of Judah to roar again!

And I can see that God is moving; people are starting to get angry at religion and passionate for Jesus. There is an unleashing of God's power taking place within his church: the prophets are prophesying, physical and spiritual pains are being healed and men and women from the most unlikely of places are creating an army ready for battle: armed with compassion, truth and a love that dispels all fear.

What keeps me going is the faith that there's more of God than we have at the moment. I read about Peter healing people with his shadow or Paul posting his anointed handkerchief . . . and I realise just how much I have boxed the 'unboxable' God that I worship. Can you see the dry bones coming to life? Even in your late age does your heart groan with me for more?

Slowly but surely, there's a hunger rising in this nation for something more, something that satisfies. I look around the clubs I go to and watch as countless people search for the unobtainable ultimate night and I lie awake at night and hear the hurt: kids fighting, families feuding and lonely people weeping. The sounds they make seem to rise up as a prayer in the night pleading along with my heart for God to visit this nation in power again.

So this is my hope for the future: that not just I, but we, the church would be humbled into seeking the fullness of Christ again. And I hope this for the sake of our dying nation.

All my love and respect,
Chris

From: Rob Frost
To: Ronald Frost
CC: Andy Frost; Chris Frost;
Subject: Looking to the Future

Dear Dad, Andy and Chris,

Your testimony about retirement, Dad, is an inspiration to me. All your life you have been striving toward 'what's next', and you continue to be focussed on tomorrow rather than yesterday. Your life is a living example that vocation is a constantly unfolding adventure. You were recently renewing your camping certificate for the Boys' Brigade, which meant pitching a tent, camping alone in the woods and cooking breakfast. Not bad for a sprightly eighty-three-year-old! You prove that God hasn't finished with us whatever age we are . . . and that there's no ageism in God's kingdom.

I guess that all of us, at our different stages of life, are all excited about living for Jesus, about discovering our destiny and of finding our place in Gods promises. Andy and Chris, with their passion for God's Kingdom and vision for revival are a constant challenge to me. It's easy in mid-life to seek a kind of comfortable compromise . . . not expecting in the future what we haven't seen in the past. But they are constantly urging me to move out of my comfort zone . . . and I'm deeply grateful!

I believe that God is doing something new. For a long time the generations have been distant and even at war with each other. Misunderstanding and mistrust have spoilt our relationships. Among the rising generation I find a real desire to reach out to those who've gone on before, and to find new ways of working together. We have much to learn from each other, and much to do together that we can't do alone. I pray that this new unity across the generations will become a hallmark of the emerging church.

I hope that this book will help other kids, parents and grandparents to tell their stories too. Wouldn't it be great if lots of people wrote across the generations to share their experiences of Jesus? And who knows what rich things we might gain from each other? I hope that our stories will encourage others to press on toward their destiny . . . and to find their place in God's promises. For this is not just something for one family . . . I believe that it's God's perfect plan for everyone!

God bless,
Rob

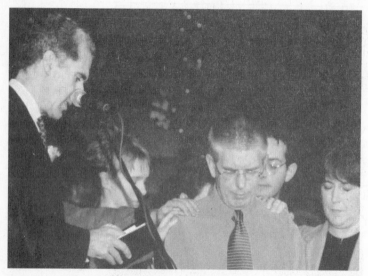

Nicky Gumbell prays for Rob Frost and his future work as an evangelist.

From Jacqui Frost
To Andy and Chris
Letter from your Mum!

Dear Andy and Chris

I always wanted to be the mum of girls but I thank God that he put me in a house of men. I am very proud of all the four men who have contributed to this book but I recognise that all your stories are 'by grace' and not the result of any of us 'getting it right'. Looking back over

'I always wanted to be the mum of girls.'

the years, things could have turned out very differently, and if anyone reads the book and feels that they have failed . . . then I'd like to make it really clear that we all have too. I recognise that grace is available for every individual, for every family and all your stories illustrate that.

I was reluctant for you, Andy and Chris, to become full-time church workers and even prayed '. . . only if they have no other option, Lord.' I thought it showed weakness to follow the family tradition and not carve your own path but now I'm really glad because I think it takes guts to follow Boss and Dad and I know that it's God motivating you both. I believe that God is doing a new thing and turning the generations towards one another in honesty and truth and that we are all a part of this 'move'.

There will be tough times ahead for both of you and probably little security as understood in society today but if Jesus remains your focus, I think the e-mails from Boss and Dad make it clear that you'll always live a rewarding, abundant life. Keep searching after God, keep your expectations Spirit-filled, keep your focus on Jesus – he's the only one who'll be there 100 per cent for you.

In a race the baton is passed on from one contestant to another and in a way the mission of proclaiming of God's kingdom has been passed on from one generation to another of the Frost family. Although faith is always a personal response to a loving God, there is a sense of a 'faith-filled' heritage which I believe is based in prayer. Andy and Chris, you have a precious ancestry and I am praying now for the generation yet to come – I pray that they'll have a passion for Jesus. One day we'll see revival, one day we'll see Christ return, one day we'll enter into eternity. Wow!

Lots of love – Mum xxx